PUBLISHED BY COPPER MOUNTAIN BOOKS

ISBN:

eBook	978-1-963781-01-4
Paperback	978-1-963781-00-7
Hardback	978-1-963781-02-1

First Edition

wishing on rainbows

A MEMOIR

LAURA SILVEIRA

Dedication

To Marcus, my best friend, my love—thank you for always encouraging me to live life to the fullest and for showing me that every occasion can call for a little Guns N' Roses.

To Bree and Matthew, my greatest gifts, I love you with everything I have and I hope your lives are filled with endless music days.

To Chase, my oldest son and angel, thank you. I'll never stop loving and listening.

CONTENTS

PROLOGUE

I AM WRITING THIS BOOK for my son, Chase. I feel kind of selfish saying that because he's in Heaven and you're the one who's holding these pages in your hands, for which I am forever grateful. But there's just too much pressure when I think about writing this book for you.

I'm Chase's mom and so by default, even if I say too much, to the point of total embarrassment, he has to love me. Plus, I don't even think you can get embarrassed in Heaven, so there's that.

When I think about writing this book for you, the river of uncontrollable fears starts to flow.

Maybe this is too much? I'm too much.
What if this is more upsetting than helpful?
Should I put a joke here? Wait, this shouldn't be funny.
Am I the only one who thinks human interaction as it
collides with grief can be kinda funny?
Am I the only one who feels awkward?
What's the right amount of laughing and crying?
Is there a formula?
I think I'm just making things more awkward.

Maybe you have a son or daughter in Heaven, too. Or maybe you know someone who does. More than likely your child didn't die at the same age or in the same way that my son, Chase, did. Maybe you're still extremely angry. Maybe you're wondering when you'll stop crying every day. Maybe you're starting to feel less emotion and that scares you because it feels like you're losing all over again. Heck, maybe you've even laughed and now you're doubting your sanity.

I don't know your circumstances, but I want you to know that I'm here. I'll be here as you're feeling all of it. Just like a bee sting (except infinitely worse), you initially feel the pain intensify and you wonder when it will stop getting worse. You worry it won't ever stop. Meanwhile, any onlookers can be seen wrinkling their faces at you as if to say "Oh, that sucks," because they can tell you're in pain, but they don't know what to do about it. Not to mention they're most likely feeling grateful it was you and not them.

I'm here to tell you that you'll get through the awkward encounters, figure out how to dodge some of the "sad eyes" and shriveled faces people throw your way, and at some point you'll know that you should feel really, *really* proud of yourself when you start to genuinely smile and laugh again. For the record, it's totally cool if that happens on the first day of your loss. There is no "too soon." Glad we got that outta the way.

I want so badly to say the right thing. I want to be able to read your heart, find even just a small corner of your hurt, and take some of that sting out. I want to take away your pain by saying lots of profound things, like I have life with grief all figured out, and leave you feeling, well, better. But I can't do that. At least not in that way—for several reasons:

I have a natural tendency to make things awkward.

Figuring out how grief fits into your own life is anything but a linear journey.

You can, you are, and you will take your own sting out. I know you will.

When Chase passed away I would have loved to have stayed in my house for years. The idea of closing off all ties to the outside world would have been glorious. I could have spent days, even months or years, working on my mental health, getting better (whatever that means), avoiding people's "sad eyes" every time Chase would come up in conversation (more than likely by me), skipping small talk, and only emerging when I felt ready, as a polished butterfly.

But that wasn't an option.

Adulting involves responsibility, something called "income," trips to the store for food (before grocery delivery existed), talking to people, and navigating general societal pressures to not be a total recluse.

So I dove into all the things. And let me tell you, it was clunky, awkward at best, and I hated it.

I'd leave most conversations immediately recapping in my mind how they could have gone better. How could I have protected myself more? How could I have made the other person feel better about my pain? It's like I was trying to push myself forward with every step even though every part of me was screaming not to. Some days just ended up feeling a little bit (or a lot bit) backwards. They were anything but linear and any control I thought I had was quickly washed away. There was no Point A to Point B. It was more Point A to Point B, back to A, then A.5, reset at 0, and then you do the hokey pokey and you turn yourself around. Okay, no hokey pokey—at least not at the beginning.

Rainbow Babies

I first heard the term "rainbow baby" from another mom who experienced child loss. If you aren't already familiar, "rainbow baby" is a term used for a child born after the loss of another. I loved the idea that there was a definition for a baby born after

3

the loss of another. If a definition existed, it meant I wasn't alone, right? Having babies after child loss happened frequently enough that someone thought, "Hey, we should really give this a name." So yes, while also sad, it gave me hope.

One night several years after first hearing the term, I called home on my way home from work. My husband, Marcus, answered. At the time, our two younger kids (our rainbow babies born after the loss of our son) were three and two years old. Marcus's voice echoed. He's a loud guy in general, but by the echo and the splashing in the background, I could tell it was bath time.

"How's it going?" I asked.

"Oh, ya know, just juggling rainbows over here," he replied.

I started to smile and knew that was going to be the name of my blog about child loss and rainbow babies. Now the blog has grown into this book that takes rainbows a step further.

My rainbows are my kids, but this idea of rainbows has grown into so much more for me. I believe that we're all getting through life wishing on rainbows. Finding the things that make us smile on the best days. Clinging to the things that keep us going on the tough days.

And just like with rainbows, they don't have to be the constants in our lives. In fact, I'd say that most of the time they're not. They can be found in unexpected moments. However brief, they leave our hearts just a little bit warmer.

Some of the gifts we gain from the tragedies in our lives can be pretty awesome. An awkward or dark sense of humor and the ability to get someone else's grief-stricken view of funny. Yup, rainbows.

I'm definitely not of the notion that life is all rainbows. Life can deliver up some pretty good piles of poop. But I believe that there are rainbows meant for you, and I want so badly for you to discover them. Or at the very least be open to the possibility.

So here I am, writing this book and maybe, just maybe, planting a rainbow meant to be discovered by someone else. By you.

Scribbling Masterpieces

Life after loss initially shaped up to feel like a messy scribble on a page. The kind where you're coloring so fast that eventually your hand slips off the page and you wind up drawing on the desk. I think there's a saying that no two snowflakes are the same. Well, in the world of grief, no two scribbles are the same. My journey of getting to know life with grief is different from yours.

As your hand slips off your page and onto your desk, I'm the friend who's here to tell you that what you're creating is a masterpiece. Yes, even the part of your drawing that slips onto the desk. Even if the only color you want to use right now is black. I like black. Isn't there a saying that black goes with everything?

The goal of these upcoming scribbles is to make you feel less alone in the awkward, the sad, the funny, the unpredictable, and the unplanned moments of life with grief. So as it turns out, in writing for Chase, I am wholeheartedly writing this book for you. The added bonus is that Chase will be proud of me. Not just by default, but because I am and always will be his mom.

While we're on the topic of grief's messiness and knowing that this book is my big chance to flex my honesty muscle, I have a confession to make. When I was creating the book outline, I was so focused on the ways in which my life and the way I parent have changed since Chase passed away that I left out a very beautiful and crucial piece...Chase's life. My mind immediately told me that I was a horrible mom who has zero credibility to write anything remotely connected to parenting. This clearly meant I

5

wasn't even grieving the right way. Once I shoved the unhelpful thoughts to the side, I began sharing everything that I hold so close. Even if it's not right, who am I to judge? I suppose I'll let you do that. I hadn't forgotten to share about his life, I just had to loosen my grip a little bit in order to let it out.

Sharing memories of those we've lost, with others, means being faced with the uncomfortable. Sad glances, awkward silence, unwelcome comments. A lot of times I'm not in the mood for the other person's discomfort. It steals some of the happiness away from my memory. Not forever, but for some time. Sometimes after I'm done sharing, someone else chimes in with a story of their child from last week, and I'm reminded that my share was from almost a decade ago and that's where my catalog of Chase's memories stopped. I hate that the well-intentioned efforts of others can make me so sad.

Feeling regret after I share Chase with people stinks, so over time, I've become guarded. I hold the moments of Chase's life so close to my heart it's hard to share them even when I want so badly to speak his name. When I keep them to myself I can find every bit of the amazing within each memory. I can sit in my thoughts and I can be there again, with him, even if only for a short while. When I share some of that amazingness, I get worried that the recipient of my gems won't understand the magnitude of it all. Maybe I'll just get a polite smile and nod. Or maybe they'll say something like, "I'm so glad you have that memory." Which is a fine response, I guess, but not the response I expect when I've just shared something that means the world to me. There aren't any follow-up questions because no one wants to make me upset.

So sharing has become less free-flowing sometimes and more sticky. Like when you try to slide across a slick floor like

Tom Cruise in *Risky Business*, but then realize that your feet are too clammy, your socks are too wet, or like me, you've lost all confidence in your coordination. So you end up looking like a stick shift car on the first day of drivers' ed.

While sharing can be awkward, these stories of Chase's life are also where I can go to find my footing. They are tangible pieces of him and our family. So even while feeling guarded and awkward, I am clinging to the memories like they're the only things keeping my feet on the floor. If I let go, I'll float away, and the time in my life where I was a mother to Chase here on Earth will seem less real.

When it helps you find your footing, even through the pain, please share your memories. You know how magical that time was, and when it's right, in a special moment, there will be an audience who knows that just as much as you do. I do. Share about that breastfeeding class and the world's greatest nip slip because there will be laughs and joy in the memory, no matter how many times you share it and even if you have to shove a heaping pile of sadness to the side. It is your footing that matters. Hold it close when you need to but sometimes try to risk it not going as planned. Someone will stick their big fat foot in their mouth. Or maybe they won't say anything at all. Don't let the worry of how others may react make you so guarded you doubt if you should say your child's name.

Share the memories and say their name. Let's start with Chase.

CHASE ROBERT SILVEIRA
Born: January 5, 2013

ONE - CHASE'S LIFE

"I CAN'T REACH DOWN TO smell it, so you have to smell it."

Life is strung together by moments of unpredictability. Moments that make you take a deep breath, look around and think, "Well, I didn't see that coming." Being pregnant and having a baby is an excellent example. I never would have guessed that my water would break five weeks early and I'd be building a pool of amniotic fluid on my bathroom floor, let alone that I'd be strongly encouraging my husband to smell it.

I'd heard stories of moms who thought their water broke and they were going into labor, only to discover they had just peed themselves. I wanted to be certain that this was my "go time." So with a dash of encouragement and the forceful tone of Nike's "Just Do It" slogan, my husband's nose was headed toward our bathroom floor.

"It doesn't smell like anything."

I wasn't sure if that was a compliment—that my pee doesn't smell that bad—or confirmation that it wasn't pee. Regardless, I was still leaking all over the floor and the shock of it all was starting to set in. My legs were starting to tremble uncontrollably. With the flexibility of a tree trunk, I waddled over to the toilet and sat down. My husband, Marcus, had disappeared to the other room to get the contact information for the hospital. He emerged quickly with a manila folder (cell phones with digital record-keeping weren't quite an addiction yet) and started looking through the pages inside. In hindsight, a manila folder just seems silly. File folders are for keeping things organized. This moment was nothing but chaos. Our bathroom looked nothing like an aisle at Staples. The tile floor and bath mats were wet and a well-fed pregnant lady who had inhaled a Taco Bell Mexican pizza just hours ago was involuntarily shaking on the toilet. That manila folder was about to end up in the filing cabinet that was our dusty bathtub as we prepared to head to the hospital.

We arrived at the hospital and I sat down at the admissions cubicle with a wet towel awkwardly draped around my waist. The sound of squishing flip-flops announced my arrival to those nearby. Yes, I was a little bit embarrassed as the motion sensor doors parted to welcome me. But I was also hoping the added visual would speed up the process of being admitted to a room. I'm not sure if it did, since I had nothing to compare it to. This was my first time delivering a baby.

Right on Time

Our son, Chase, was making his entrance into this world five weeks early. Just a few hours earlier Marcus and I had actually been at this very same hospital for our first birthing class. I'm sure that completing the class would have been super helpful, but the first night was more of an introduction and I had learned nothing. Actually, that's not true. I learned that I should find a really comfortable pillow and bring it to next week's class. My fluffy pillow was now a wet towel. Practically the same thing.

Once I was checked into a room, I actually ended up crossing paths with the nurse who was teaching the birthing class. Technically, I was just lying in bed when she walked in. I jokingly told her I wanted a refund and then kindly asked for the CliffsNotes version of her teachings (not joking). She reassured me that I'd do a great job, which really meant it was too late and I'd figure it out. If I was going to try and learn something new at this point, I'd be passing with a C at best. Luckily that first night at the hospital was pretty uneventful as far as a delivery goes. I had plenty of time to stew in my own thoughts—because that's always helpful (insert heaping pile of sarcasm).

The next day my doctor arrived to check on me. He smiled, asked how I was feeling, and stuck half his arm up my who-ha. My face was awkwardly smiling, while my mind was thinking, "Son of a b*tch!" There was a certain level of concern that my water broke and delivery was still moving slowly. As uncomfortable as this all was, it was nice to see a familiar face. I was preparing myself for some quality doctor-patient time, possibly some Q&A. Maybe a pep talk. Instead, that's when he told me he was going out of town for the weekend and I'd be in great hands.

Ummm, what? What was more important than being in this room? I was selfishly thinking, "Is your golf game really that important? Do the bride and groom really need you there?" Maybe I would have let it slide if he told me it was his Broadway debut. Even then I felt like I was the one who would be deserving a standing ovation at the end of all of this. I never did find out why he couldn't be there. Honestly, I was so surprised and disappointed I didn't even ask. And, as swiftly as he'd arrived, he left.

While the doctor may have been on his way out, there were others on their way in: My mom, Linda, who had arrived from out-of-state, and my mother-in-law, also Linda. Both had plenty of time to perfect the art of chair sleeping. The nurses called them "The Lindas." I've since memorialized this as a term of endearment along the lines of "the Lindas are so loving and funny." Not "oh, great, here come the Lindas again."

Through the comings and goings of the nurses and the Lindas, Marcus was right there with me. After that first day I'd been given some Pitocin to try and speed up the contractions. Marcus was sitting on the edge of the bed, holding my hand and watching the monitor for approaching speed bumps. At one point his grip loosened and I took it as a sign that I was getting a little bit of a break. Okay great, flat road ahead. To my surprise, a contraction came and it was anything but a slick surface. I looked over to read Marcus's facial expressions, except I couldn't see them or his face. His head was facing downward, resting on the edge of the bed. He had fallen asleep. I could hear some heavy breathing through the beeps of the monitors, which eliminated any doubt.

Although I'm not a big sports fan, I've picked up a few basic concepts from being married to one. Stay safe, support your team, and...don't fall asleep at second base? I just assumed that last little nugget was a given. (To be clear, I'm talking about baseball, not the other kind of bases. Get your head outta the gutter.) In anticipation of "go-time," (again, baseball) Marcus had taken some of his anti-anxiety medicine. To ensure he was feeling the calming effects by the time I graduated to the pushing portion of this event, he'd stepped it up with an extra dose. How many times had he tacked on an extra dose in the past? Well, once if you count this time. In his defense, both of us had anticipated that all of this delivery business would happen a lot quicker. Keeping the sports analogy going, I asked one of our coaches (the Lindas) for a time-out to take my favorite player for a walk. Time to regroup and then get our head back in the game. At some point it would be time to push.

My Longest Shift

I didn't start pushing until Saturday. If you're keeping track, we entered the hospital on Wednesday night. Pushing started out as more of a questionable hobby. I wondered if I was doing it right. My body wasn't really feelin' it, but we were now several days out from when I had wet the floor of my bathroom. The intensity of the delivery process increased in tandem with the size of the audience in the room. It felt like someone had challenged the hospital staff to see how many people could fit into one of these labor and delivery rooms. I've never tried crowd surfing at a concert but this would have been a great time to give that a try. I don't think there's a more trusted crowd than nurses, right?

At one point my bare booty was facing the hospital room door and an older female nurse was holding my leg up. She had been on shift for a while now and I was glad she was sticking with me through all of this. She had a very nurturing grandma vibe. While she had my leg, the rest of my body was facing my husband on the opposite side of the bed. He was definitely occupying the quieter corner of the room. I heard the nurse instruct me to roll my body over to face more in her direction. My head rolled over first. It was the only thing that didn't feel heavy and tired at this point. To my surprise, my leg was now being held by an older male nurse. When did he get here? Crap, where was nurse grandma? Her shift was apparently over and mine just kept going.

Amongst all the noise of the nursing shift changes and the rumbling of medical equipment carts, it suddenly became very bright in the room. Very, very bright. One of the concertgoers—I mean nurses—had turned on a searchlight of some sort. My eyes squinted as I tried to adjust. Uh oh, had we lost someone in the crowd? For the last several days I'd felt more like a quiet observer, but if anyone was lost, I would have been happy to join the search party. The idea of not being the center of attention seemed a little appealing at this point. Or if everyone was present and accounted for and they were simply on the hunt for my vagina, I could have very easily guided them in the right direction. I hadn't been able to see that girl for months, but I was pretty sure she was still down there somewhere.

There were several nurses standing in the background, with their hands calmly clasped together. They had that "quiet observer" role down pat. They were standing next to the little cart where Chase would hopefully be placed soon. I was informed this was the NICU staff. Chase was making his debut into the world five weeks early so they just wanted to be on the safe side. This was the first time it even crossed my mind that this could be a delicate situation.

I was tired. The searchlight was warm, and it was now highlighting the blood vessels that had popped in my neck from all the pushing. The Lindas had to be getting tired of pacing the hallways. It had literally been days. Marcus was being so supportive even after I'd lovingly asked him to get out of my face at least once. All kidding aside, I was truly grateful his anxiety meds had worn off many hours ago.

With a few more strenuous pushes, encouraged by the voice of a stand-in doctor saying "one more" several more times, Chase was here. The room got quiet. Chase was quiet. The strong voices that echoed in the room a few minutes earlier were now talking in whispers as they moved him over to the cart and the awaiting NICU nurses. It had only been seconds, but we couldn't see him anymore. A few moments later we heard his sweet cries. And then we cried. The doctor reassured us that even though he'd arrived early, Chase wouldn't need to go to the NICU, and he'd be staying with us. We took this as permission to fully enjoy the moment. Everything was okay.

Forehead to forehead, my husband and I smiled through welled-up eyes and looked at each other. Actually it was way more than a look. We locked eyes, feeling the sweet weight of the situation. Our love had brought life into the world. We had a son. We had *our* son. The frequency with which we'd hear our proper names, Laura and Marcus, would forever be less and more frequently replaced with Mom and Dad. I used to think that the scene in *The Lion King* where they hold up the baby cub was a little dramatic. At that moment, a gesture of that magnitude didn't seem inappropriate. In fact, I might say it seemed necessary. But maybe I'd wait to give it a try until after I'd had a nap and a sandwich.

I still lock eyes with my husband. Partially because he has really big eyes and they can lock you in like laser beams. It's also because I think I'm trying to jump back into that moment at the hospital when we were forehead to forehead. When the nursing crowd around us was dissipating and we were starting to feel the weight of our first few moments of parental bliss. Usually, when people start leaving the party, it's a sign that it's ending. Not this time. The love was growing by the second and we just couldn't all fit in the room anymore. It was now a mostly empty space that felt full and warm even after that dang searchlight had finally been turned off and put away.

There was a break in the lovefest as we were kicked out of the labor and delivery room and moved to the recovery floor. Let's call this the after-party. This was still a place of immense love, but it also came with a heavy dose of logistical confusion for us parental newbies. We learned to change diapers, button up onesies, and figure out the difference between a poop cry and an I-just-want-to-be-held cry. It was a lot. I have those cries too, but Chase's were his own.

Settling into Motherhood

The confusion and learning continued even after we were discharged from the hospital. I'd missed that birthing class but I'd also missed the free breastfeeding class. Actually, I'd missed the birthing class, but I'd been avoiding the boob class. A few days into parenthood, though, had me realizing I needed to avoid my avoidance. The hospital had given me a referral for a class that was regularly held somewhere downtown. A few days into breastfeeding I decided it definitely wouldn't hurt (oxymoron) to get some helpful nips...I mean, tips.

Marcus, Chase, and I arrived in the parking lot, and we sat in the car for a few minutes to mentally prepare. I was jealous that Chase was sleeping.

"Are you sure dads are supposed to go to these things?" Marcus asked with hesitation.

"Why wouldn't they be invited? Plus, I don't want to be the only one having to take notes. This is a little overwhelming." I snapped at him like he was trying to be an absentee father.

We were a little early (the first and last time this ever happened in my early days of parenthood), so we decided to go in and get settled before class. The class was being held in this cute little house that had been converted into a lactation services office. The living room was where the class would be held. In a room off to the side (once a dining room?) I could see a scale and some equipment to take baby measurements and get more one-on-one time with the consultant.

We headed into the living room. The room was free of chairs but there were lots of pillows on the floor. We put Chase's car seat down on the outskirts of the cushioned area. I gently unbuckled him, hoping that I wouldn't wake him up from his slumber. Wrapped in some blankets, I picked him up and the three of us found our space on the floor. A nice lady saw us criss-cross apple-sauce to take a seat and reassured us we were in the right place. Marcus and I were looking around like skittish cats. He was looking for more dudes to show up and I was already trying to find the quickest way to an exit. I have always been pretty modest. Locker rooms make me uncomfortable, and for the better part of my teen years, I made my mom wait outside the dressing rooms when I needed to change. So the thought of seeing a boob, even mine, in a room full of ladies had me on edge. I was taking these few minutes to try and get my head in the game.

Other moms started to show up. Some of them were talking amongst themselves. This was a weekly class so some of them had been here before. They were definitely looking more comfortable than us.

They made their way to the living room floor, where a circle was starting to take shape. It was closing in. I looked over at Marcus, still the only male in the room, and I looked at the clock on the wall. There were only a few minutes before the class was about to begin. I gave him the nod. The nod that says, you have my permission to get outta here as fast as you can. He looked so relieved. All I heard was, "I'll be in the car" as he began his sprint. I not so jokingly replied out loud, "Take me with you."

I've never been a part of a drum circle, but I'm guessing it would feel like this. Except we didn't have drums. We had boobs and babies. The nurse joined the circle and class was in session.

She asked the frequenting moms how it was going and she asked us new moms to introduce ourselves. Of course I was the only new mom that day.

"Hi, my name is Laura. This is Chase. He is five days old and I have no idea what I'm doing. Thank you." I've always had a way with public speaking.

I looked down at Chase, hoping that the mention of his name didn't spark him to wake up and join the party. All I kept thinking was that if he wakes up, he'll be hungry. If he's hungry I'll have to try and feed him. Yes, I know, that was part of the class curriculum, but we're not all going to excel at every subject. I wasn't aiming for valedictorian here. I just wanted to take some fully-clothed notes and leave.

Shortly after introductions, it happened. The boobs came out. Not mine, thank goodness. I tried my best to seem very breezy about the whole thing. Don't stare. Smile so you don't look like a weirdo. Give off the vibe that you too feel that this is all a beautiful and natural thing. Keep your eye on the parking lot to make sure Marcus hasn't left.

This was the longest parenting hour of my life so far. Once the drum—er, breastfeeding—circle was over, we were all invited to stay as long as we liked. If we wanted updated weights for our baby, or had specific questions we still needed addressed, we could wait for a turn in the other room. We all started to stand up, and while others looked like they were nestling in for Part Two, I was trying to pack it up as quickly as possible. I think that was enough areola for one day. No, I was not the class valedictorian, but you know who was? Chase. He had stayed asleep the whole time. "Mommy loves you" was on repeat as I exited that nicely repurposed home to meet Marcus outside in the getaway car. You are correct, that was our first and last breastfeeding class.

I wasn't always the passenger of our getaway car though. At some point I found my way to the driver's seat. Like when Chase and I had our very first play date. I'd like to take this opportunity to say that playdates are the world's cruel way of putting unnecessary pressure on moms to show each other that they have their mom sh*t together. I do not.

I went into it feeling pretty confident, so I'm not entirely sure how it all went so wrong. The day before said playdate, I had mentally prepared. If Chase and I had to be out of the house by 11:00 a.m., that means I would have to wake up five hours earlier, at 6:00 a.m. This would give me plenty of time to shower, get dressed, feed Chase, feed me, pump, clean pumping apparatus, poop (me, then him?), get him dressed, pack the diaper bag, get ourselves in the car and arrive at our destination. Shoot, maybe I should make it 5:00 a.m.

The morning of the playdate things were going well. I had checked all the to-dos (and doo-doos) off the list. I placed Chase in his car seat and gathered up the diaper bag, which I'll admit was overpacked. I probably should have made a couple of trips to the garage to pack the car, but I'm one of those people who tries to unload all the groceries in one trip. I stepped out into the garage with my arms and hands chock full of necessities. Before I could even figure out how to start opening the garage door, I heard the noise of the back hatch of our car and I watched as it started to open. I didn't even have the car keys in my hand. How was this happening? I looked down at Chase, resting in the car carrier in the crux of my arm, as if to ask him if he opened it. This was not going to be good.

The hatch was opening and the garage door immediately behind it was still closed. I realized the car seat was pressing up against my now sweaty thigh, where the car keys were inconveniently placed in my pocket. I guess technically Chase *and* I had worked together to open the back of the car. I dropped the diaper bag in an attempt to free one of my hands and press the garage door button on the wall. If the garage door could open at a faster pace than the car hatch, we might avoid a mini garage door collision. But the crunch I heard next confirmed that I did not avoid this little fender bender. The hatch met with the garage door and the car got the worst of it. I was able to close the car hatch (another crunch) and get us over to the play date. In the end I was about twenty minutes late to the playdate, frazzled, and sweaty. I made a detour to an auto body shop on the way home for a quote to fix the hatch.

I've Got This—I Think

Things were in a state of emotional flux with Chase for the next six months. We were in this beautifully ignorant emotional state of "Yup, I totally got this" to "Nope, I actually don't got this—at all." I'd go back and forth between moments of pure happiness and moments of wondering if I was doing anything right. I would joyfully stare at Chase, all swaddled up after another fun bath time. Next thing I know, I'm yelling for help when an unexpected poop had gone up his back and through my fingers. Then I'd spend a decent amount of time wondering if the color of his poop was normal.

Being a new parent is kind of like making a stiff, fancy drink. Once it's all mixed together it looks really beautiful. The ice cubes swirl around the glass, making the sounds of wind chimes. There might even be a citrus peel curled up for decoration or a sprig of lavender. Whatever branch you throw in there, it's going to bring you so much joy. Then you take a sip and your face shrivels into the shape of a raisin. You feel your nose hairs start to burn as you wait frantically for some of the shock to wear off. You start to question yourself. You did everything the recipe asked, so how could something so pretty taste like nail polish remover? When you're a new parent, you keep trying to perfect the recipe and hope that the results burn a little bit less each time.

I feel like I can't talk about the joy without being honest

about the really hard times. Made even harder now that he's gone (yup, I'm getting there). Most notable was the time that I passed him off to someone else.

About a month after Chase was born, Marcus's extended family was in town for an annual weekend celebration. Marcus was golfing with his brothers, uncles, and cousins. I had decided to take my time getting ready that morning and join up with the family later in the afternoon. That was the plan until I heard my doorbell ring. I answered the door and saw Marcus's sister and his cousin's wife standing there. It took me a few minutes to adjust to the change in plans, but I was happy to see them. This was another opportunity to show that I had this mom thing all figured out. But I didn't. I was tired, constantly doubting myself, feeling a little lonely, and pretty overwhelmed. I was still wondering when that whole "routine" people talk about in baby books was going to show itself.

All it took was one of them to ask how I was doing and I melted. We were standing in the kitchen and I was carrying Chase tightly in my arms. I could feel my arms start to get heavy as my tears welled up. I asked if one of them could take him for me. I felt like a failure. What kind of mom passes off her child? One of them gladly scooped up Chase for some cuddles while the other instructed me to take a seat on the couch as she opened a bottle of wine. A moment of loneliness can feel like a lifetime until something or someone reminds you that it's not. It felt so good to feel less alone.

This memory about letting Chase out of my arms stings. I want so badly to be able to say that I held him every opportunity I got, but I didn't. I hope he knows that mommy was trying her best even when the results were kinda sad, because a lot of times, in all the unpredictability, they were funny.

Sweet Baby Giggles

I remember the first time that I made Chase laugh. I had placed him on our bed so that he could excitedly watch me fold laundry and I could enjoy his chubby baby rolls. Okay, maybe he wasn't excited, but there is no doubt that folding underwear was made 1,000 times better for me because he was there. I propped him up against one of our large pillows. The one covered by a large sham that I often questioned why anyone would ever need. That day I needed it to keep sight of him over the mound of warm clothes I'd just brought over from the dryer. As always, a piece of clothing managed to escape off the top of the fresh cotton mountain. I bent down quickly to pick it up and popped right back up. That's when I heard it. The first little giggle. I looked over at Chase just in time to see the grin fading from his cheeks. *Was that what I think it was?* I "dropped" a piece of clothing on the ground again, disappearing from his sight for another quick moment. As I sprang back up, I looked immediately at him so that I could catch the beginning of that smile. I heard it again! Only louder this time. And I caught all of that beautiful smile in the process. Our first game of peek-a-boo, although completely unplanned, was a success. I yelled for Marcus to come into the room and he tried it too. Success! We even managed to catch it on video for all the naysayers who think we're not that funny. Chase was the best audience for our literal stand-up career.

Six Glorious Months

One of my last big memories with Chase was the weekend before he passed away. We were taking family pictures with my side of the family. We had traveled down to San Diego to visit my brother's family and be with my parents. We knew it was our first big road trip. We didn't know it would be our last. A photographer came to the house and we took so many pictures. Chase with his cousins, grandparents, aunt and uncle, and with us—Mom and Dad. I am forever grateful for these photos that capture how big my baby boy was getting. Plus it's really nice to have some pictures that aren't the product of my blurry and caffeinated hand.

I spent a magical six months with my son. Between the chaotic nurse shift change on the night of Chase's arrival and the family photo shoot the week before he passed away, we learned a lot together and covered a lot of topics: feeding schedules, tummy time, sleeping routines, learning to laugh, and being cool with crying (from both of us). I loved where we were at and I wasn't done yet. Not even close. But that wasn't my choice.

Along with all the magic, there were the missteps. I want so badly to be able to say that these six months were perfect. That I never had to yell for help or question things or hand him over to someone else. That I swaddled with the skills of an origami expert. But that would all be a lie. So my hope is that Chase looks back at these moments in an endearing yet very realistic light. I hope the total picture results in a resounding "mommy loves me."

TWO - HE'S GONE

I REALLY WISH LIFE CAME with intermissions. When things are going great, you could use it to catch your breath in between laughing spells. When life is confusing, you could take a few minutes to evaluate, or ask some clarifying questions. Or when life shatters you into tiny pieces, you can take a much-needed time-out. I know we're only on chapter two, but I'd like to propose a bit of an intermission.

I want to share about the day that I broke into tiny pieces. I need to. How else can I encourage you to keep going if you don't know where I started from? While this was hard for me to write, it's not lost on me that this may be hard for you to read. How many times does someone bring up a story and you immediately think, "That's just like the time _____ happened to me"? We're connected by our stories. We're connected at a deeper level by the stories of our broken pieces. Please know that I'm wrapping you in an extremely awkward hug—the kind where you'd like me to let go, but I take that as an opportunity to just squeeze a little bit harder. Please take as many intermissions as you'd like. Life may not always allow for them, but I do.

Give Me Some Knuckles

I will always remember the last morning that I dropped Chase off at Brenda's, our daycare. It is one of my very special memories with him. I believe the universe gifted it to me so that I could hold onto something in the tough days ahead. I climbed up the stairs to the front porch, with the car seat embedded into my elbow crease and Chase resting comfortably. It was a clear morning and it was just the two of us. The neighbor down the street owned a few horses. I could hear their faint whinnies as they enjoyed their breakfast. I held onto Chase in his carrier.

With less than an arm's reach between us, I looked down at him while we waited for Brenda to come to the door. He looked up at me with his big brown doe eyes. He seemed like he had something he wanted to say to me, but at six months old, I'd have to wait a little while longer to hear it. So instead, I did the talking. I told him I couldn't wait to talk to him and I hoped he had a great day. I looked down and saw his wiggly, pudgy fingers resting on his lap. I reached down and gently held his hand, my thumb combing the dimples that would eventually be his knuckles. The moment was interrupted as the door swung open and Brenda accepted him with a huge smile on her face and the "Good morning, baby" I'd grown to love so much. I moved his car seat inside the door and put it down. Brenda and I chatted for a few minutes, covering all the important stats before I headed off to work—last feeding, last poop. That was our last moment. That was our goodbye.

This Can't Be Real

Chase passed away later that day on Thursday, June 27, 2013. Near the end of my work day I was sitting in my cubicle, preparing to leave shortly to go pick up my mom at the train station. She was coming from Oregon to California to visit us. By "us," of course I mean Chase. Sure, Marcus and I would be there, but I'm sure she planned to give him most of the snuggles. Chase, that is, not Marcus. Although Marcus loves hugs too.

As I was getting ready to shut down my laptop and pack up my belongings, I received a text message from my husband. It wasn't too profound. Actually, it was the exact opposite of profound. It came over as just a blank bubble, like he'd thought about typing something out but then decided against it and accidentally hit send anyway. I could have left it alone and dismissed it altogether, but I started to wonder if he knew something I didn't. My mom's train was delayed? He'd be coming home late tonight? He needed me to pick up Chase from daycare? I wrote back with a simple "?" and I was prepared for a short text exchange to follow, but what I got back instead was the call that would change everything. Everything. Life. Meaning. Parenthood. Faith. Trust. Self. Relationships.

I picked up my husband's call and, in true fashion, I was getting ready to cut him off before he started. I hate that I have a tendency to do that, but I get points for acknowledging it, right? I was going to tell him that I was on my way to the train station. A slight exaggeration since I was still staring at those cube walls. I could hear him breathing. It was infrequent and heavy. Then I heard the sound of his voice. For a few moments it wasn't words, but sounds. Like he was trying to catch his breath and talk at the same time. He was struggling to get it out. As I heard his first real words, I could feel myself slowly starting to rise from my chair.

"He's gone."

As my husband released tears, I stared blankly over a largely quiet maze of even more cube walls. The conversation had just started, but I felt like I was playing catch-up. I wanted to be where my husband was both emotionally and physically, but all I could do was stand there.

Marcus was at the daycare. I needed to get there. He said the sheriff's office was sending a car, but I didn't want to wait. I told Marcus I'd figure it out and I'd be there soon. I hung up the phone. Crap, this was getting logistical. Going from point A to point B was going to take way more thinking power than what I had in me. Some of my coworkers were still around and had started to realize that something was wrong. I took a small U-turn around my cubicle wall and saw their quiet and concerned faces. I'm not exactly sure what they could pick up from just my side of the phone conversation, or exactly how loud I was talking. I have a reputation for being a pretty loud phone talker. That, coupled with cutting people off as they start to talk are among my finest qualities. They had looks on their faces that made it seem like they almost knew more than me. They already looked sad for me. Part of me was thinking, if they look this sad and surprised, what the heck does my face look like? Because it wasn't until seeing them that it started to become more real. As I started to talk, someone swiveled an office chair over to me to encourage me to sit down. I started to bend my legs but part way to sitting I stood back up with conviction. If I get down I don't know if I'll get back up. I think I actually said that out loud. If I don't sit down, maybe the horribleness that was unfolding wouldn't have someplace to land. Maybe this will be less real. Maybe it'll all just stop.

The Longest Ride

My coworkers helped me gather my things and coordinate my ride to daycare. My manager drove me in my car, and another car followed to take him back to the office. Right before leaving, another new mom reminded me that my breast pump was in the company's makeshift mothers' room downstairs. A small fridge held whatever milk I'd managed to squeeze out between meetings that day. I paused, not knowing how to respond. About thirty minutes earlier I would have been panicked at the thought of forgetting to bring my milk and pump home with me. "Just leave it. I don't think I need it anymore?"

As the words came out of my mouth I quickly realized how abrupt they sounded. My life was nothing but abrupt in that moment. Chase was here. Now he's not. I was so lost already. There are so many times in grief that I've had an opportunity to show myself some grace. I can look back at this moment and think, "Why the heck would you say that?" Or I can think that I'm really sad for this fairly new and scared mom who doesn't yet understand the magnitude of what's still to come.

As we started the drive from work to daycare, my boss was arranging mirrors and getting acclimated to his new ride. I had assumed the role of passenger seat blob, but my mind was racing. I still didn't even know what had happened. What if something went wrong? What if there had been an accident? Should I be mad instead of sad? Should I be making phone calls? Should I call my in-laws? Should I call my parents? Crap, my mom. The train station.

I called my mom and told her very matter-of-factly that Chase had passed away and we needed to get to daycare. I asked her if she could find a ride from the station. I felt like I was breathing fast and talking even faster than I could think. Like stages of grief, are there stages of shock? I'm pretty sure there are. I'm evidence. After talking in circles and practically encouraging my mom to hitchhike, it started to settle in how much I wanted my mom, and we made a turn to the train station to pick her up. Actually, it was lots of turns. I couldn't remember how to get to the station even though I'd been there dozens of times before. I was able to confirm on that day that my car does pretty well at off-roading. We made it to my mom. I introduced her to my boss as she climbed in the back seat. She was very quiet.

I did make the call to my in-laws, after confirming that my husband had not yet. They were traveling in Arizona at the time. My mother-in-law picked up the phone. I could tell they were in a car too. I probably should have advised them to pull over. Like when I told my mom, my words were inappropriately blunt. I wanted to make sure our parents knew before I got to daycare. My mother-in-law was in disbelief. Hearing her try to process what I'd said was sad to hear. She was trying to ask questions but her voice sounded as if it wanted to cry out at the same time. I don't even remember how the conversation ended. There's not a "right" way to break horrible news. It's just horrible. Which is why it's never going to feel "right" coming out of your mouth.

It had only taken me about thirty minutes that morning to drive from daycare to work. That night it took almost an hour to get back. We approached the dead-end road where Brenda lived and I instructed my manager to make the next left. I couldn't figure out if I needed to take one last deep breath, or hold it all in. A rush of questions came into my thoughts. What is this all going to look like? What should I prepare for? What happened? Where is Marcus? Will I be able to handle what's coming?

Taking this drive to daycare had been such a comfort over these past three months. The time I had in the car with Chase every morning before work was our time. I would talk to him about playing nice with the other babies while giving myself lots of high fives for making it out of the house on time. Okay, almost on time. Almost is great enough, dammit.

My car turned the corner and the unknown picture in my head came into focus. There were quite a few cars parked on both sides of the road. I thought they would be marked as local law enforcement, but they were more discreet. It would soon start to sink in that this was an investigation after the fact and not the scene of an accident. There was no ambulance or flashing lights. I had missed the busyness of trying to save him. Chase had passed away around 3:30 in the afternoon. It was now about 5:30 p.m.

As we pulled up closer to the house, I pointed to a stretch of dirt and gravel on the side of the road to park the car. I could hear the crunch of every piece of gravel under the tires as the car rolled to a stop. I saw Marcus. He was sitting on the curb out in front of Brenda's house. His legs were curled up and he sunk his head into his hands, looking down at the nearby cement. There was a straight-faced sheriff standing over him. The front door of Brenda's house was wide open and people were coming and going. Besides the sheriff taking post out front, these people weren't dressed in full uniforms. I could tell they were here on official business, though, by the various combinations of badges, lanyards, and an occasional pair of stiff cargo pants. I missed the normal after-work shuffle of parent pick-up. I'd always exchange polite smiles with the other parents, knowing that after what were presumably long days away from our babies, coming back here was the best part of the day. Where were the other parents and their kids?

Marcus must have heard the gravel from my car tires. He lifted his head up from his hands in slow motion. I imagined that he'd looked up several times before thinking it was me, only to be disappointed with the appearance of another stranger. He rose to standing and started walking out into the street to meet me. I stepped out of the passenger side of the car and as soon as I got around the front hood to a clear breakaway, it became my mission for him to be in my arms. Not that I didn't need to be in his, but for the past hour I had been surrounded by people I knew. Friends and colleagues who wanted so badly to help me. I had my mom. And Marcus had been here with no familiar face, waiting for almost an hour. We grabbed hold of each other like we were each other's life preservers. We were. We stood in the middle of the street hugging. We'd been in this embrace many times before as we've been known to love a good dance floor. But this was different. My arms were so heavy. Just like those dreams where you're being chased and you can't run fast enough. I couldn't squeeze hard enough. My arms were so heavy I couldn't grip as hard as I wanted to. I could hear his muffled cry in my shoulder, penetrating every cotton fiber of my shirt.

I wasn't crying. Why wasn't I crying? What the heck was wrong with me? Yes, shock definitely played the largest factor here, but for someone who's known to be an (overly) emotional being, this was beyond out of character. Maybe that was it—denial. It wasn't me. It couldn't possibly be me.

So Many Questions

As we eventually lowered our arms and silently agreed to put space in between us, I could see past Marcus's shoulder to the large group of neighbors looking at us from across the street. I wondered how long they'd been standing there. They were just staring and occasionally leaning over to whisper to each other. Did they see me looking back at them? No one turned away to even try and pretend that they hadn't just been caught. No one's ever apologetic for looking at a really bad accident.

My manager and coworkers were still standing by my car. They were looking at us too, but with concern and a thoughtfulness in their eyes. I walked over to thank them for their help and let them off the hook. I told them they should go home. I'd shared enough trauma with them for one day and I knew we'd be talking more in the days to come.

I returned to Marcus, who filled me in on what the past few hours had been like for him.

He had arrived at Brenda's to pick Chase up as he did every day. He knocked on the front door but instead of seeing Brenda's petite frame, a large-statured sheriff answered, asking Marcus to confirm that he was Chase's dad. The house was split-level. The front door opened to a small square landing with one staircase on the left leading upstairs to the main living area and one staircase on the right leading to the downstairs, which was designated for the daycare.

Driving on instinct and panic, Marcus charged forward to go down the stairs on the right side of the landing to see Chase. He didn't get very far. The sheriff quickly grabbed hold of him and pressed him up against the wall. He wasn't allowed to go downstairs. Marcus pleaded to see his son. As his initial burst of energy faded, the officer was able to slide Marcus down the wall and into a seated position on the tile floor beneath him. Marcus sat still and he could hear Brenda, her husband, and her teenage daughter crying hysterically upstairs. He headed outside to get some air. That's where I would find him waiting for me.

Marcus and I stayed outside for a while. My mom had started making some phone calls at my request. I'm sure she made a few of her own. I'm not exactly sure when she told my dad, who was still at home in Oregon. The officer outside tried his best to walk us through what was happening and what he knew, which wasn't much. He did assure us that there didn't appear to be any wrongdoing. Chase had fallen asleep for his nap. Brenda's high school-aged daughter went to go check on him just a short time later and he was face down and not breathing. Brenda tried to administer CPR but it was unsuccessful.

I asked the officer how Brenda and her family were doing.

"Not good at all," replied the officer. He said we'd be given an opportunity to see them later, if we wanted to. I told him I wanted to. I didn't really know if I wanted to. What I wanted was to not be doing any of this. I knew my heart needed to see them and I felt like their hearts needed it too.

He explained that someone would be out shortly to ask us some questions. After that and once they'd gotten all the pictures they needed inside, we'd be able to see Chase. I asked if this was the only time we'd be able to see him again. The officer said there may be a chance later, but he wasn't quite sure where Chase would be located after the autopsy.

The autopsy? I nodded like I understood what he was saying, but on the inside I went further into confusion. "So, I'm sorry, they're going to cut him?" The officer looked at me, expressionless. I know I can be extremely awkward at times, and by the glare the officer gave me after those words came out of my mouth, I knew this was no exception.

"I'm sorry, is that a weird thing to say?" I asked.

"Yes." he replied. I realized at that moment that I was probably a suspect in his eyes. To think that I had something to do with Chase's death...well, I couldn't even go there. I guess we were both trying to make sense of what was going on, but his approach sucked. For a split second I wondered if this was all my fault. I'm still mad that the officer made me feel this way and at myself for being apologetic in our exchange. If anyone was wondering why I wasn't handling all of this like I "should," it was me.

A woman, Shari, came out of the house to talk to Marcus and me. She was a detective with the coroner's office. We'd be talking a lot to her over the next several weeks. I liked her. She didn't make me feel weird. She was kind and it felt like she was there to help our family. She asked us a few questions about Chase and that day. Had he been sick? Had we given him any medications? Does he have Down Syndrome? Um, what? To be clear, it wouldn't have mattered either way, but being that this was never something that was brought up by medical professionals after he was born, I was caught off guard. I should have asked her why, but I just replied with a simple "No."

I couldn't help but think back to my pregnancy with Chase. I'd had some genetic screening and the results had come back indicating a higher probability that he could be born with Down Syndrome. We spent time with genetic counselors and, after having a more extensive ultrasound, we were told that it didn't seem to be the case. So when Shari asked again, I felt like something had been missed. I was so confused. There is so much that is unknown when you're pregnant and now I was realizing that death wasn't exactly a clear picture either. Questions were bringing up questions.

Going Inside

Feelings of confusion subsided as soon as we were allowed to see Chase. We just wanted to be with him. Shari prepared us. She told us that we would be brought downstairs to spend time with him. It was now a few hours since he had passed away, so she warned us that he might feel a little cold and rigid. We would get as much time with him as we needed. Once we were ready to leave, Shari said she would be taking care of him. He wouldn't be in the back of their van or alone. She'd have him wrapped in a blanket and would carry him in her arms as a baby should be. I thanked her. She may have thought I was just thanking her for a twenty-minute van ride, but I was thanking her for her overall kindness in such a delicate situation. I was thankful that the questions were over. I was thankful people had stopped coming and going. I was thankful for some quiet. And I was also afraid. I wanted to see Chase, but I wasn't ready to say goodbye. What if I didn't do this right either?

We were led into the house and down the stairs. It was quiet. I'm guessing someone had told Brenda and her family that we were coming into the house, because the only thing I could hear was silence. Which is why I was surprised, as we stepped off the downstairs staircase, to see a handful of officers still standing around. I felt like we were on display even though everyone seemed to be avoiding eye contact. I tried making eye contact with the strangers, but there were no takers. I wondered if this was protocol or just more evidence of the social awkwardness that death brings. Either way, I did kinda appreciate it. I think they were trying to make this as much of a "private moment" for us as their jobs would allow.

Marcus and I sank down onto the tan leather couch. The same one we'd seen every day for months. Shari came over with Chase wrapped in a white sheet to lay him in my arms. At first all I could see was his fluffy head of soft dark hair poking out. There he was. My baby.

As she bent down, I could really see him, and he was so beautiful. He was back in my arms and it felt so familiar. "Hi, handsome," I said softly. That is the moment my tears started. The moment I realized he was gone. Finally, I saw a glimpse of myself again as his mom and an emotional being.

Marcus, Chase, and I stayed on that couch for quite some time. If there was ever a time in my people-pleasing life to not worry if I was lingering for too long or putting people out, this was it, and I took it. We took turns holding him and talking to him, like when he was first born. We knew how amazing it felt to

36

hold him and we didn't want to keep the other one from savoring our last pieces of this magic. We told Chase we were so sorry and we told him that we loved him so much. We held his hands and kissed his little lips and forehead so many times. I could feel his soft little face starting to get cold just like Shari said. With parental instinct we'd adjust the white sheet every so often to make sure we had him wrapped up as best as we could.

My mom was standing in the corner of the room. I think I asked her if she wanted to hold him. Mom, I'm so sorry if I didn't. At some point during our goodbyes and cuddles Marcus and I realized this wasn't going to get any easier. Once we were both in agreement, we told Shari that she could take him. It felt like when he was alive (just hours ago) and we were just letting someone else share in the joy of holding him. The reality that we wouldn't be getting him back wasn't something I could comprehend in that moment. That is exactly why I'd asked that officer standing outside if we'd get to see him again. Shari leaned down and cupped her arms to cradle him. We placed Chase down into the cradle and picked up the hanging sheet over her forearm to rest it over his perfect little body.

Someone asked if we'd like to see Brenda and her family. I nodded.

Hours earlier Marcus had been an audible witness to their distraught cries. They had been placed on the upper level of the house and had been waiting there this whole time. I had no idea what to say to them. I was not mad. I was at a loss—for words, and more. I was trying to understand how the death of my son had changed someone else's life on top of mine. Marcus and I slowly walked upstairs, unsure of how this was going to go. We didn't have to walk far. Brenda, her husband, and her daughter met us at the top of the staircase. We sat there in a cluster on the floor. We just hugged and cried. Actually, I think they cried, mainly. I couldn't support someone else's weight at that moment, but I knew that I didn't want them to feel abandoned, wondering if I was angry in any way. Or if I blamed them, because I didn't.

Going Home

We eventually stood up to leave. We didn't say goodbye and there were no promises exchanged to see each other soon either. It was very noncommittal—a quiet goodbye with a caring hand squeeze. We walked out of the house and into our separate cars. Just us. Marcus into his car and my mom and I back into mine. It had become a habit for me to take a quick look in the backseat and at Chase's car seat, before starting to drive. It was my "is everyone ready to go?" check-in. I looked briefly at the empty car seat base in the backseat. Marcus, my mom, and I took the very long and very quiet five-minute drive back home.

Once home, Marcus and I crossed paths in our bedroom, putting car keys in their place and changing out of our work clothes. The bedroom was lit only by the light in our bedroom closet. It wasn't for ambiance. We'd already started to question the meaning behind lots of things, like turning on lights. We stood there, on a small matted-down patch of carpet in our bedroom, and we hugged. I told Marcus that no matter what comes next, we need to keep checking in with each other. A marriage after a child dies is the kind of thing that statisticians do research on. What's the percentage of marriages that end after a child has died? Heck if I know. I mean, I have looked it up. I've also repeatedly ignored their results. It's not us. This isn't a statement of denial (okay, maybe a little), but we literally have not been part of a study, so technically it's not us. I wondered how many people we knew would hear the news and comment, "Geez, that's horrible. I really hope they make it."

As I was learning to battle all the thoughts in my head, I honestly didn't know what Marcus was thinking that night, and there would be lots of moments like this to come. Even if I didn't know what he was thinking, it was more about me just wanting him to know that I was there.

Marcus's oldest brother and his wife showed up at our house later that first evening, after driving several hours to get there. Marcus's mom had called them knowing that she couldn't get to us just yet. I don't remember saying much, but we all just stood in the family room. I think we recounted a little bit of the afternoon's events. This was the first time I'd see people we loved wanting to help but not knowing what to do or say. I felt bad that they had come all this way. They had a place to stay in the area, so after they left, we decided to go to bed. I wondered if I'd even sleep. I eventually did. Of course, only after I posted to Facebook.

The past six months have been the best of our lives... because we got to spend them with our handsome son Chase. But God must have bigger plans, because He took you today. It must be bigger than we could ever imagine, to make us feel this much hurt. You'll always be our perfect boy. Mommy and Daddy love you more than you'll ever know. We love you buddy.

I blamed myself.

If I hadn't been at work and needed daycare for Chase, maybe he'd still be here. He wouldn't have been taking a nap at their house. He wouldn't have gone to sleep in *that* crib on *that* afternoon.

Nope, don't go there, Laura. What's the "better" alternative?

If I didn't work, Chase would have been napping at home with me. It would have been me who put him down in his crib and it would have been me who found him and frantically tried to remember CPR. I would have called Marcus to tell him that Chase was gone. People would have been coming in and out of our house. It would have been our neighbors staring. We would have said goodbye to Chase in his nursery.

And then there's the version where I wonder if he'd skipped his nap altogether that day, then maybe he'd still be alive.

Is there ever a "better" version of blaming yourself? Definitely not. So I lean into what I know. Brenda and her family carry those final frantic moments so that I don't have to. And for that I will forever be grateful. I am grateful that she was there for Chase when I couldn't be. I'm grateful she was there for Chase when I wasn't.

Wasn't? Or couldn't be?

I'm careful with my word choice because I have to be careful with this mom heart of mine. "Wasn't" makes me sit in blame and punishment. "Couldn't" allows me to be part of the club of "bad things happen to good people."

If I *wasn't* there, then I let Chase down. If I *were* there, I could have saved him.

If I *couldn't* be there, well, life just didn't allow it. It happened to me, not because of me.

So which one is it? With a good dose of hindsight, I'd say both. Hindsight is the "should have." If I'd known that my son would die at daycare, I *should have* never gone back to work after he was born and been more attentive.

A Possibility of Joy

Over the years I've been asked if I feel guilty at all for Chase's death. After silently thanking the person asking for bringing up a sensitive and loaded question that implies I should feel guilty, my short answer is usually, "No, thank goodness" as I explain the burden that Brenda lifted from me. But I think I'm lying to myself a little bit. She's not carrying the full burden. She was there and wasn't able to save him. I wasn't there and...well, that's it. I wasn't there. Even if I don't feel overwhelming guilt, like I'm dragging around a huge boulder all the time, I do carry some guilt around. Maybe it's more of a pocket full of rocks. They can fall out on occasion so I feel a little bit lighter about how everything happened, but I eventually pick them back up and shove them into my lint-lined pockets.

I'm not going to make it my life's mission to punish myself for the *couldn'ts* or the *wasn'ts*. And I don't really know what to do with people's overly abundant reassurance that it wasn't my fault (aggressive enthusiasm just sounds a little "blamey" to me sometimes). Probably best to follow my lead as I work through all the emotions. I reserve the right to dabble in guilt, circle back around to just plain sadness, and even stay open to the possibility of joy. Yeah, I said it—joy.

Joy vanished the day Chase died and I wasn't in a rush to find it. I was incapable and I didn't want it.

The road back to wanting anything other than your child back is so lonely. There are moments you'll feel like you're the only one on Earth to feel this much pain. No one around you understands that you are forever changed. You are different to your very core. It almost feels out-of-body because you can't even figure out who you are or what the point of anything is. Looking in a mirror isn't necessarily the most fun activity. In fact, wearing a name tag when staring at your alleged reflection might be helpful. I'm not a scientist, but I would go so far as to say that when you're in the depths of your grief, your DNA actually changes. It has to, right? Because how else can you feel like you're saying goodbye to the person you were and entering a world of starting over to discover who you are now? I look back at the girl I was in college or the happy bride on my wedding day and I think, "That girl was so happy...poor thing had no idea what was coming." She was someone else. That's not me anymore.

The moments you don't feel alone you feel so crowded and everything is so loud. Life is happening for other people and you're just there.

So where do you go and how do you get there? The days will come and you will be there. At the beginning, that's enough. *I repeat, that's enough.* I don't want to give you a quiz later but I will if that's the only way you'll hear me on this one. You don't have to do anything but be. That in and of itself is a step.

THREE - THIS IS GOING TO BE ROUGH

I WOKE UP EARLY THE next morning and slowly walked out to the family room. It was so quiet. Way too quiet. Marcus was still in bed. I thought I was the first one awake, but my Mom was already dressed and I could smell coffee. She'd talked to my dad on the phone. He was starting his road trip across state lines to our house, and she was more than likely bracing herself for a busy day of being, among all other things, my communications director. As I walked out of the bedroom and through our short hallway, we met. She looked at me and I looked at her. That's all it took for me to start crying.

I wasn't crying as a mom who had just lost her child, but like a daughter looking at her mom for a way out. I didn't want to do this. I didn't want to play anymore. This wasn't fun. I wanted her to make it all better. It reminded me of when I was in grade school, terrified to give a speech. I wanted her to tell me I was off the hook and she'd call in sick for me. I wanted approval to get out of facing my fears. We knew it wasn't an option, both then and now. I know she would have definitely phoned it in for me on this one if she could. The hurt I saw in her eyes was knowing that she couldn't, even though she wanted to.

On top of the emotional heaviness of the beginning of the first day, I was now in physical pain. My boobs were engorged with milk and my breast pump was at work. Yup, the one I said I didn't need any more as I had left the office in shock. Just

43

wonderful. And by wonderful, I mean the absolute furthest thing from it. In a small way, I think I knew this physical pain might be coming and was hopeful that it would distract from the emotional weight of the situation. Well, that time was now, and let me tell you, my girls hurt like a b*tch. As a new mom I knew at some point I was going to stop breastfeeding, but all the baby books described a lengthier process. The chapter directions weren't simply "Just stop."

My mom grabbed her car keys and drove to my office to get my breast pump. A work friend who had already heard the news of Chase's death let her into the building. My mom came home and told me that people were just really sad for us. I know I couldn't have emotionally handled stepping back into that office so quickly, and I know it couldn't have been easy for my Mom either. The next several days were filled with letting the tatas fill up to physically painful levels (again, kinda on purpose), pumping, going to the sink to clean said breast pump parts, and pouring milk down the drain. Yes, I know, breastmilk can be donated and I commend the mamas that take those steps to share, but I was in loss mode and leaning into thoughts of pain and emptiness. In reality, it was more of a free fall than a lean. *I was skydiving into grief.* Watching the milk go down the drain was my life's metaphor at the time, so that's what I did. That's what I was capable of. Staring at the drain.

Embrace Your Beautiful Capabilities

Do you ever feel like sometimes being "capable" has a negative connotation? Like "you are capable of so much more" implies somehow that you're not applying yourself the way you should be. Or when you express to others what you're capable of, you feel like you have to dress it up a little and add some flair in order to avoid people giving you a look of "umm, that's it?" Yeah, I hate that too.

Entering this child loss club was the first time I was very aware of what I was capable of. Learning how to embrace that, whatever "capable" looked like for me, was downright glorious, and an important lesson. Getting out of bed? In the words of Charlie Sheen, I was "winning." Starting a load of laundry? Go to the head of the class. Attempting to have a fully-focused conversation? The Academy Award goes to: me. Some days probably wouldn't look impressive to others, but that doesn't matter anymore. When you go through something that changes you, hurts you, or changes your life's course, the focus should be about embracing your own capabilities. Your own beautiful capabilities. If you're capable of getting dressed, awesome. If you're just thinking about opening the front door a crack to remind yourself what the sun feels like, but you wouldn't dare step outside... amazing. Eventually it can look like more, and I truly believe it will, but it's more than okay if that's not where you are at. Where you are at is perfect. Climbing Mount Everest is for show-offs.

I wasn't prepared for visitors, but it wasn't long before they came. I was surprised, grateful, and scared. I was appreciative of the support, but I was also nervous to have company. I hate being the center of attention on a good day. How would this feel on a sad day? Would they look at me like that judgy sheriff from the day before, wondering how I'd act? Maybe like I'm a lost puppy, with compassionate sad eyes? Or like I'm contagious and they don't want what I have. I wouldn't blame them. When something bad happens to someone, we all do a little bit of a "not it!" game, grateful that it's them and not us. I'm fully aware that I may have been overthinking this a little—but *only* a little bit. "Human nature" is unavoidable in uncertain times.

Marcus's childhood friends were the first to arrive at the house on Friday—the day after Chase died. They walked in and we exchanged hugs. Stepping into hostess duties to avoid talking about anything, I offered them a seat. I think all I could handle at the time was politeness. Open door. Welcome guest. Offer them a seat. Look at me go! As I looked to our small family room, I realized space was limited, and Marcus's friends formed a larger crowd than I had remembered. I needed to make room. That's what hostesses do. As I did with leaving my breast pump at work, I looked around at Chase's things, still set up near the couch and saw what I didn't need anymore. The bulky baby swing. Before I had time to think I told his friends that we could move that out of the way. I realize now that this probably made them uncomfortable. I think someone actually asked if I was sure. Outer dialogue was a "yes, it's fine," but my inside monologue was screaming a big "please, no." After I offered the words of reassurance about my decision, I could feel myself breaking a little bit more inside. I didn't check with Marcus before I said it. I wasn't trying to be selfish; I just didn't want him to be worried about me and my ability to make hard decisions. A painful decision. Should I have left the swing out for a little bit longer? Would staring at it, empty, have been less hurtful? I'm not a gambler, but this grief stuff has a bit of a roll-the-dice element to it. Make a decision, see where it lands, and figure out if you want to try again. The swing was picked up and moved into Chase's nursery and I asked for the nursery door to be shut—another roll of the dice. I didn't know what kind of relationship I had with that space anymore, so the easiest thing was to not look at it for now. I also didn't want to be reminded of what I'd just done.

The guys decided to go to the store for a few things. They asked if we needed anything specific. I placed an order for cigarettes. Not one cigarette. *A carton.* My mom was in the kitchen washing dishes. She heard my request and looked over. The last time we'd talked about cigarettes was when I got busted for smoking in high school. There was no disappointment in her eyes this time. It almost felt like she understood where I was coming from. She calmly said, "You don't need those."

Sometimes there is a very fine line between "need" and "want." At that moment I think I could have argued this debate— and maybe even eventually won. Not because of my great talking points (because cigarettes *are* bad for you, kids), but because my mom was grieving too and we would have probably reached a point of exhaustion that ended in, "Fine, do what you want." But there was nothing victorious to be had here. I ultimately decided I'd save my bad choices for when I was alone. If I wanted to hurt myself more I'd just do it privately. That was my plan. I told them to forget the cigarettes—for now. Once Marcus's friends returned from the store, they visited for the rest of the afternoon and then headed back home. We knew we'd be seeing them again soon once we had a funeral figured out.

Meanwhile, my brother was driving north from San Diego. My niece was less than two months old at the time and I felt bad that all of this was taking him away from his own life's beautiful busyness. Having to sit in this much of my own grief was new for me and I would handle it. But upon seeing my brother drop what he was doing, too, I felt like a burden. As quickly as he arrived, I wanted to tell him to go home because all this fuss was unnecessary and I was fine. I thought if I showed my big brother that I had it all handled, he wouldn't need to worry. Maybe I could fix his own grief over losing his nephew. Sometimes the little sister is the one who wants to have it all taken care of too, ya know. Yes, I realize that all my thoughts at this time were delusional. I couldn't fix anything. We were all starting our own path with grief and sometimes the paths put us in close physical proximity.

Venturing Outside the Cocoon

Marcus's parents arrived the next day, Saturday. They had driven straight through a few states to get to us, leaning on the phone calls of friends to keep them awake during the late hours. I was glad they were here for us, but I was mostly relieved they were here for Marcus. I already knew what it felt like to have my mom close by. The first time they saw Marcus, they quietly leaned down over him, embraced, and cried. I slowly stepped out of the room to give them this time. They needed it and Marcus needed it. Marcus quickly melted into being a son who needed his parents more than being a father who lost his child. I didn't know my husband growing up but it felt like this was my best glimpse, minus all the troublemaking.

Our home had become our cocoon. I'd say "command center," but that implies efficiency and planning. Marcus and I didn't have the capability for either one of those attributes. Yes, even though home was way too quiet, held endless reminders of our son we could no longer hold, and felt oddly smaller now with one less member, it was still a safe place. Or a *safer* place, at the very least. It felt much safer than going outside. Although I'd hoped the world outside had stopped, I was aware, at least at a very high level, that it was still moving. I knew life outside would bring many challenges, most of which would be out of my control—as I had now been made painfully aware.

The first time Marcus and I ventured out of the house we took a walk around the block. We were perfectly fine inside, but the Lindas thought it was a good idea. Our moms were back together and instead of pacing the hospital hallways they were manning our cocoon. We reluctantly put on shoes. Or, in my case, flip-flops. The toes gotta breathe, right?

Do you remember the *first* time you went on a roller coaster? Someone probably dragged you to go on it. You spent minutes pumping yourself up with encouraging thoughts like, "Lots of people do this and they always come back to the station." Yup, not exactly embracing a thrill of excitement. It was more of a "let's get this over with so my friends will leave me alone" feeling. That's how Marcus and I felt about this walk.

We hesitatingly left the house, greeted by slightly unwelcome sunshine. I checked my pockets, verifying that I wasn't bringing anything with me. It felt like a voyage I should be better prepared for. Keys? Cell phone? Swiss army knife? You're right, the keys and the cell phone would have been overkill. We reached the sidewalk and immediately held hands. Here we go. One foot slowly went in front of the other. I didn't realize there was so much that went into a casual stroll. Left leg, right arm. Right leg, left arm. Don't forget to pick your head up and look around. Maybe a glance over to the neighbor's trees and flowers. Geez, this was a lot. Then it happened. We saw someone up ahead, walking their dog in our direction. This is the part of the roller coaster when you can see the climb up to the top of the large drop. You try to remind yourself of your breathing and not to look down (or forward in this case).

There's already something awkward going on when you pass someone on a walk. You want to look over and acknowledge them, but if you do it too early, you wind up staring and you'll come off as creepy. Do it too late and you'll come across as unapproachable and rude. Marcus and I both felt the pressure. As the walker got closer, Marcus and I lifted our heavy heads.

We cracked a soft smile and said "hello." Phew. We had done it. We had made it through our first "casual" encounter. Check that box. We rounded the remaining corners of our neighborhood block and could see our house approaching once again. This was the only time I felt like going into a full sprint. I had the urgency of Jodie Foster trying to make it to the panic room. I didn't act on it, though, largely because I wasn't emotionally capable, but also because there were flip-flops involved. We eventually made it back to our cocoon.

If successfully getting through our first casual encounter with someone was like the peak of the roller coaster, the feeling afterwards should have been one of release, right? A deep breath followed by an almost satisfying stomach drop. The wind in the hair explained not only by sheer speed, but also by a large gust of accomplishment. But this walk wasn't a satisfying accomplishment. We were both well aware that this was only the beginning of the ride and there would be more peaks and steep drops ahead. Again, as life had just shown us, ones that we wouldn't even see coming. But one flip-floppity foot in front of the other, literally, was as good a start as any.

Every Step Counts

I sometimes wonder why a walk around the block has stuck with me for so many years, cataloged in my memory as courageous. It was just a walk, right? Like, in the world of grief, am I throwing myself one of those "everybody gets a trophy" parties? Well, maybe. But a large part of me (now) knows this isn't true. Walks are hard, especially when your feet feel like they weigh 500 pounds. Every step counts. Even the missteps. We had managed a few steps forward that day, but the next day brought us backwards.

Marcus chose that next day, Sunday, to try and escape it all. Marcus, his parents, and my mom and I were all together at our house. It was a pretty quiet day. We were still waiting for my dad to arrive and we were in limbo with the funeral planning since the autopsy was still pending. I was still busy mastering the art of doing nothing so I wasn't keeping close track of what Marcus was up to. "He's around here somewhere" would have probably been my most accurate response to his whereabouts. That afternoon, I was sitting at our kitchen table with my mom when I heard noises coming from our bedroom. I walked in to find Marcus looking dazed and sitting on the side of our bed. I thought maybe he'd just gotten up from a nap and was a little out of it. He went to look over at me, but instead, his eyes were focused on anything but me. And why was he swaying? He slowly got to his feet, took a few stumbling steps around me, and started traveling toward our bathroom. We never made eye contact. He wasn't capable. He hadn't been taking a nap. My best guess was that he'd been drinking—a lot. Before the moaning and vomiting started, I asked for his parents. They came in and I went out.

Prior to seeing Marcus, I had been at the kitchen table, being encouraged to try and take a bite of a sandwich. I wasn't hungry but I knew taking a bite of a sandwich would be more of a victory for those around me. I just had to decide if I was going to do that for them. Like so many times in the past few days, I just sat in indecision. So my ability to help another human being, even Marcus, someone I loved with all of my being, was nonexistent.

Now back at the kitchen table, I could hear whispers from his parents as they were taking care of him. I'm not sure if they were talking to him or to each other. I'm pretty sure he lacked the capacity to absorb any advice or jump into a conversation. Marcus had been gulping wine like water and had used it to

51

wash down a heavy dose of his anxiety medication. Definitely not a prescribed dosage. I feel like I should tell you that I was mad at him for handling things this way, but I wasn't. I was actually more disappointed. I felt disappointed that I didn't take the gulps with him and generally mad that I understood the feelings of wanting to take away pain in such a destructive way. I didn't have the emotional capacity to help him, but I understood. I think others did too. When his brother arrived a few days later, he told Marcus never to do that again. He didn't. We didn't talk much about it, but I knew he wouldn't.

I anticipated that the next day, Monday, would have Marcus nursing a horrible hangover and maybe some regret. I was way off. He showered, got ready for the day, and then announced that he'd be redoing the mulch in the whole backyard. Um, wha'? His cousin had come to visit. I'm pretty sure his cousin hadn't antic-ipated manual labor upon his arrival. Marcus wanted the yard to be ready for visitors after Chase's funeral. Even though we didn't have any details sorted out, Marcus was adamant that we'd be hosting a memorial gathering at home rather than renting out some sort of event space. I was okay with people standing on old bark, but hey, you do you.

As he and his cousin were getting on yard gloves, I was back at that kitchen table playing a new game of "will she eat the sand-wich?" If I was ever interested in going on one of those nature survival shows, this would have been the time. I would have been a contender for the grand prize. A feeling of nothing left to lose, a suppressed appetite, and a desire to sit in my aloneness would have been positive attributes for those contestants. Except I wasn't sitting naked in a jungle. I was three days out from the death of my son and I was supposed to be planning a funeral, or, as they say, "making arrangements." I wasn't making squat.

My dad arrived from Oregon. The last time I remembered seeing my dad really sad was when my grandma passed away when I was in high school. From a man who's mastered the art of holding in his sneezes, I knew the sadness I'd seen even back then was muted. So I was anxious thinking about what this sadness would look like for him. What if he finally decided to let the full sneeze out, so to speak? Through the blinds I saw his car pull up in front of our house. I quickly went out to meet him as he was walking across our front lawn. I didn't want him to feel on display once he came inside. As I could now confirm from walking into daycare for the last time with lots of eyes on me, I've felt the spotlight and I'm not a huge fan. We hugged a few yards from the front porch. There were some tears, but I'd say they were muted for both of us. I've always considered myself a "crier" and chalked it up to taking after my mom. To be clear, I have become very proud of my ability to show and share emotion in my life. But thinking of this particular moment, there's an element of comfort that I'm also my dad's daughter.

Sometime later, my sister-in-law, Melinda, walked through our front door. She and my brother had agreed that he would come up to see me before the funeral, while she stayed with their kids. That was the agreement—until it wasn't. She told me she couldn't just stay home. So her mom stayed with the kids and she drove up. She walked in the front door and looked like she'd been crying for the entire five-hour drive (but of course still stunning). I stood up from the couch and we embraced. I was glad she'd ignored the plan. There were so many times I thought I didn't need people, until I saw them and realized I was wrong. I also hoped that, in some way, seeing me could help her with her pain.

No Rules

In the rawness of the first few days of grief, there are no rules. If there are no rules, then no one has the power to say what's wrong or right with how you're handling it. Yes, they still might take this as an opportunity to provide their unwelcome two cents, but please remember this truth and go easy on yourself and possibly even them if it means you can save some of your energy. To recap: everything is heavy, decisions may not be the most thought out, and the simple things are to be commended to the level of winning an Olympic gold medal. Fact: It's a slow build to feeling like you're fully functioning.

FOUR - DECISIONS I'D RATHER NEVER MAKE

T HERE WERE NINE WHOLE days leading up to Chase's funeral. My days continued to be jam-packed with forgetting to apply deodorant, hustling to perfect the art of the blank stare, and preparing to earn my master's degree in living a life that will never feel fully whole again. Though regardless of what lay ahead each day, it still needed coffee. It wasn't about the coffee itself, but about a piece of routine that I could still hold on to.

One morning I woke up and wandered aimlessly for a bit, still getting used to feeling the void of not having to go to the nursery, and then sat down with my full cup. My dad was sitting in a reading chair in our family room and I slowly settled into a couch cushion across from him. *The Today Show* was on. I think it was Kathy Lee and Hoda at the time. I don't care what people say, I kinda liked them together. I was trying to fool myself into thinking it was a treat to be home mid-morning and catching their segment, rather than at work. The reality was that I had no idea what they were talking about because I was perfecting my art of the blank stare. As the television played, I could see the energetic duo engaged in witty banter, but all I really heard was the muted wah-wahs of Charlie Brown's teacher and the downward spiral of my own thoughts.

I want Chase back. I don't want to move forward without him. Why does this hurt so much? I just want to sit here forever in my pain. Everything feels so heavy.

My arms were heavy, my heart was hurting, and I'd kinda

forgotten—actually probably didn't care much—about my coffee. Little by little, with each weighted thought stacking on top of the last, I could feel that fresh cup of coffee I was holding slowly start to lower. Around halfway through the cup's descent, I realized that my eyes had welled up so much with tears that I couldn't see a thing. Maybe that's why I could hear so clearly. My other senses were heightened. I heard my mom, who was now standing in the kitchen behind us, urgently tell my dad, "Bob, grab her cup!"

My dad got up quickly from the reading chair. Our house was cozy, so luckily he wasn't having to make a sprint across the West Wing or anything. He grabbed my cup just as I finished lowering my arm to my lap and I continued to sob. The tears that had welled up finally spilled over the trough of my lower eyelids. Maybe that's why I didn't drop the cup right off the bat— it wasn't what was supposed to spill over that morning.

You know how when you look back on your life, and it seems like it's in pictures, with some more vivid than others? This picture of me with my coffee—and then quickly without it— is something I'll always remember even when I want to forget. Was it a turning point for me? Unfortunately, no. Did I finish my coffee? Nope. I don't even know if I ever took a sip. Was I wearing deodorant? Again, highly unlikely. It is, however, a picture of my brokenness.

I wasn't *kinda* hurting. My state of being wasn't just a *little* tender. I wasn't just questioning my purpose. No. I was questioning the point of life. My life. Did I really need to be here? If I wasn't allowed to be Chase's mom here on Earth and clearly deserving of joy, then why even try to love anything? In a conversation—albeit brief—Marcus told me he had those same thoughts during this time. Yup, broken.

Healing Will Come after Sobbing Over Coffee

There is another side to this though, which I couldn't see then, but I'm grateful to see now. There isn't healing if it's not broken. I know, it may sound cringeworthy, but I promise you it's not off the mark.

Sometimes sobbing over coffee is required and I need to be proud of that rather than push it away. Who cares what I think I should or shouldn't do? Those are thoughts wrapped up in concern of what other people are thinking. It's okay to hold onto the messy pictures of life. In fact, don't just hold on. Give them a big squeeze.

I've learned to hold my own cup of coffee again (yay, me!), and I know that if I need to take a moment to sink in on the couch, it's totally okay because I know how to get up again when I'm ready. And I will. So yeah, in summary, a stroll around the block or drinking an eventual non-alcoholic morning beverage is a well-deserved, hall of fame induction kind of moment. It's been years now since Chase went to Heaven and I still celebrate the crap out of these so-called "simple moments." Healing is anything but simple or linear; sometimes, it just masks itself in simple ways. Don't be fooled by the idea of inconsequence. It's all important in *your* next right direction.

These simple moments can actually be a nice reprieve from the heavier moments that involve more decision-making energy.

Fresh or Synthetic Flowers

The worst day since Chase's death was the day we visited the mortuary and the cemetery to make the funeral arrangements. Our parents came with us. Marcus and I had collectively decided to bury Chase at our local cemetery. It wasn't so much a decision with all-encompassing conviction, but one prompted with,

"I don't know, what do you think? That sounds nice." This was a surreal experience. Not only was I faced with my son's death, but I would soon be forced to look at my own mortality.

During our time at the mortuary we selected a casket, committed to a funeral date, and got a tour of the space where the service would be held. I gotta tell you, this was the worst party planning, *ever*. Let's just magnify all my hosting insecurities and anxieties, shall we? I'm more of a potluck kinda gal. Let's all bring something and deflect from the magnitude of the gathering. No such luck here. The weight of everything was heavy as we faced these "final" choices.

When asked who we wanted to be the pallbearers, we felt really good about having all of Chase's uncles take that role. We were gently reminded by the funeral director that the casket was very small and there wouldn't be enough room for all of his uncles to hold it. That didn't change our minds. Whoever couldn't hold onto his little bed would just stand behind it. The mortuary had a really cute chapel attached that had quite a few rows of seating. I was hoping we'd at least fill a few rows with immediate family and a few friends. I imagined this is what it would have felt like at Chase's future birthday parties—hoping that a few kids would RSVP "yes."

After we finalized arrangements at the mortuary, we drove with our parents to the cemetery to select Chase's plot. A very kind groundskeeper took us around in his golf cart to show us the available areas to pick from. I'm a big fan of real estate, but this was the worst open house ever. He pointed us to an area in the back of the cemetery and told us that was where a lot of the children were buried. I was thinking how sad it is that there's an actual section. I was also relieved to think that Chase could be with other kids. Maybe Marcus and I would meet other parents when we'd come to visit. Yes, I'm fully aware that this wasn't an elementary school ice cream social or a preschool tour; however, the desire for your child to have friends and be in a safe place extends well beyond life. Also, if Mom can find like-minded parents with something in common, added bonus.

We drove back to the children's section—our section. It was peaceful. I walked around and looked at some of the surrounding engraved stones. There were other children Chase's age, some younger, some older. There were portraits etched in stone, toy cars, and stuffed animals that had fallen over into the dirt. All these trinkets looked like they'd been there for a while. There were some fresh flowers and some dirty and faded synthetic ones. I wondered how often I'd be coming here. Would I find comfort (regular attendance with fresh flowers), or just more pain (synthetic flowers to last over the moments I can't get myself to go)?

The groundskeeper showed us some numbers written in paint along the cement border of the grassy area. These numbers were to help identify the plots that were still available. We saw the number 21. This was Marcus's baseball number growing up. We took it as a sign. This is where Chase would be. Then the groundskeeper asked if we'd like to look for our own plots. Excuse me, what?

He explained that a lot of parents decide to reserve a surrounding area now so that they don't have to worry about it later. Later? Um, I didn't want to worry about it now. Plus, I still hadn't ruled out the idea of being cremated and spread somewhere. No idea where—another decision I'd rather not make. The plot right in front of #21, now Chase's plot, happened to be available. Not exactly the lottery I'd like to win but it did seem like a good score with all things considered. Our tour guide said we wouldn't have to reserve two plot numbers for Marcus and me because two caskets can be stacked on top of each other. Were we really having a conversation that shed light on cemetery efficiencies? The planner in me still wondered if we should reserve more space just in case. How do we know what "family" will look like for us going forward? The unknown shouldn't stop us from being prepared. In fact, it should encourage us, right? I was getting ready to ask for a group rate discount on buying up multiple properties when Marcus quickly reminded me that as fun as we are in life, not everyone we know will want to be buried with us and we should work with the two plots for now (Chase's and our double-decker). The groundskeeper assured us that we can always make changes, and if we decided this wasn't the right spot for us, we could sell our plot to someone else later. Wonderful—instead of house flippers, we could be plot flippers.

What's the "C" for?

As we were all driving back to our house, Marcus and I asked to be dropped off a few blocks from home. At a bar.

We had a drink, maybe two, took in some good people watching (the afternoon dive bar crowd never disappoints), and we talked about the day. We didn't get crazy and tie one on or anything. We just needed a minute. A minute to avoid life. A minute to ourselves. Another minute before being back in our cocoon. But I should have known that sadness is a welcome visitor to bars. We couldn't escape it. It wasn't like back in college when we'd make friends with the DJ and ask when the foam pit was coming out (oops, I've said too much). We had our sad drinks, paid our bill, and walked home.

A few days later and still in preparation for the funeral, my mom and I ventured out to get a pedicure. Much like the walk around the block, it was an activity that gave my mind some focus without lots of responsibility. Sit in a chair while someone touches my feet? Sure, let's give it a try. Seems like it could be something I could handle. I dealt with the outing until it became my first encounter with grief's awkward and hurtful ways. You know that feeling when someone rips off your band-aid right after you finish explaining that they need to pull it off slowly? After the fact you look at them, almost confused. You know they heard you, so *why on Earth...?* This became a band-aid moment.

My mom and I were each sitting in our massage chairs as our feet were starting to get pampered. So far, so good. I thought Chase would like blue, so that's the color I went with. I decided I needed something even more tangible than a favorite color, so I asked the man working on my talons if he could paint a "C" on my big toenail. He agreed. I spent the next few minutes trying to prepare myself in case he asked me what the "C" stood for. Now was as good a time as any to practice telling people my son died. I kinda felt bad that I could potentially ruin this man's day, so I started to silently chant, "Please don't ask. Please don't ask."

"What's the 'C' for?"

Dang it! He asked.

I took a breath and calmly explained that my son had just passed away and we were getting a pedicure for the funeral. The "C" was for my son's name, Chase. The man nodded and went back to my toes. I was a little relieved that the conversation had ended there. I talked. He listened. I slipped back into my own world. Great. That went...fine. I was a little bummed there wasn't even a tear. I mean, this was a little more than matter-of-fact news. Not even a frowny face? He looked back up at me as if he was getting ready to say something. Here it was—he just needed a minute. I was actually grateful to be able to practice comforting someone else after hearing my tragic news.

"How old are you?" he asked.

"I'm 34," I responded.

"Plenty of time to have more kids."

Ummmm, wha'? There it was. Band-aid ripped. What on Earth? I think he legitimately thought his words were encouraging. Maybe he even thought I appreciated them. Like it was a positive spin on an otherwise tough situation? I honestly don't know. But what I did learn from this encounter is that grief paves the way for people to say some really weird, rude, hurtful, awkward, and fill-in-the-blank things. I was just a bystander in the nail technician's processing of my grief. I could have given him the helpful tip to never say that to a grieving parent again, but I wasn't actually feeling like the subject matter expert on child loss less than two weeks out from the worst day of my life. I was so caught off guard, I didn't even have time to shape my reaction or response, which I'm pretty sure came off as equally awkward. A half-smile showed up on my face, and I let out a quick "yeah," as if he'd brought up a great point that I hadn't thought of before. He definitely hadn't. For the rest of my time in that chair I daydreamed about running to the car after kicking him in the face and blaming it on being ticklish (because I hate confrontation).

I truly believe that the nail technician had good intentions. I don't think his hope was to take all my pain away with one flippant comment, but I also don't think he was looking for an opportunity to pour an endless amount of salt into my gaping wounds. But there I sat, with my feet and my heart exposed to the elements. I never acted on that whole kick-to-the-face thing. Instead, I sat with my half-smile at the ready, hoping that I'd selected the quickest drying nail polish they had so my mom and I could get the heck outta there.

I've learned time and time again that I can't control people's intentions. And the interpretation of said intentions can lead to a minefield of my own questions. It's like when I played the game of telephone as a kid. Someone whispers something into your ear. Then you have to turn to someone else and repeat the whispers of what you think you heard.

"Plenty of time to have more kids."

Possible translation: "Your son was so young. You need to look at the positives and move on."

"Plenty of time to have more kids."

Possible translation: "I really don't want you to start crying in this chair so I'm going to say something breezy in the hopes that we can just stop talking about it."

"Plenty of time to have more kids."

Possible translation: "Your loss is so unimaginable that I'm going to say something I shouldn't because this death stuff is uncomfortable and I wasn't prepared for your news."

Yup, that last one is it. That's definitely what he meant. I'll never know for sure, but that's the one that makes that moment sting just a little bit less.

The pedicure outing was enough of an intro to awkward societal norms about grief for one day. I was actually looking forward to getting back home and focusing on the funeral and after-party planning. At least then I could be honest about where my head was at in a safe and supportive environment.

My sister-in-law, Melinda, had put together all the print materials for our wedding five years earlier, and now she was taking on the role of program director for her nephew's funeral. I know this may come as a shock, but I actually hadn't even thought about a program, or any funeral content for that matter. Marcus and I sat on the bed as she shared a draft of the program she'd put together. We provided input on some things, but it was more just finishing touches before it went to print. We looked at poetic verses and layout. All I knew was I didn't want anything too "churchy." I didn't know how I was feeling about this whole God business even before Chase went to Heaven. So this was really throwing a twist into things. Where the heck was He at in all of this? What would my relationship with Him be like after I spent the next several years waffling between sadness, rage, and avoidance? I didn't feel the need to give Him too much air time right off the bat. A few shout-outs were fine, I guess. Melinda coordinated a slideshow of Chase for the service also and enlisted the help of some friends with technology. I was so grateful to have a movie all about Chase for people to see. I was so grateful for all the help. Everyone was grieving but everyone else had the added element of trying to be functional because I sure wasn't.

As Ready as Possible

Since Marcus had already taken care of the new bark around the house, we were focused on other elements of having people gather at our house. As a reminder, our focus was a little off. Food? Nope. Thank you to Marcus's older brother and his wife for feeding everyone. We were more concerned about the most important element—bathrooms. Where was everyone going to go to the bathroom? Yes, our house has bathrooms, but Marcus and I wanted to keep our master bathroom closed off for us. Would one bathroom be enough? Would it be just like the casket—too small and not enough room for everyone? In this uncertain time, there's only one solution: porta potties. It would be a tight fit getting the potties through the side gate to our backyard, so we parked them on the sidewalk in our front yard.

Please take this as confirmation that we are very fancy and we know how to throw a party.

In an effort to reassure our neighbors that we hadn't turned hillbilly, I took to our neighborhood's Facebook page to send out a note letting people know the toilets and extra cars parked on the street would only be temporary and the changes would just be for the day of my son's service. With loose ends (and rear ends) all addressed, we were as ready as we were ever going to be.

After nine chaotic, quiet, loud, awkward, numb, sad days, it was here: the day we'd bury Chase.

I still wasn't expecting many people, but they came. Oh, they came. The outpouring of love and support will never cease to amaze me. I had hoped that a few family members would be at the service. Some close friends would be nice. I wasn't expecting hundreds, *but hundreds came.*

At the service, Marcus and I took our seats early. We didn't exactly have to fight for the front row and I'm pretty sure things wouldn't have started without us, but we wanted to be near Chase for as long as possible. Plus, the thought of greeting people sounded terrifying. Like the panic attack, I might break out in a weird rash and have a nervous breakdown kind of terrifying. Chase had this really soft blue blanket. It was sherpa on one side and velvet on the other, sewn together by a satin trim. We had placed another blanket in Chase's casket, so today we'd be holding onto this one for comfort. I didn't care that it was one of the hottest July days on record and it made my lap and hands wet with sweat.

We focused forward in our pew and avoided turning around. This would be the first time I would be with a lot of people. A lot of people and a lot of emotions made quite the cocktail for me, an overanalyzing and overly anxious people pleaser. I could hear the sound of people entering the chapel behind me. A friend of mine from elementary school appeared before me. To say I was surprised was an understatement. I hadn't seen her since our wedding. She had driven for hours to come.

I put down the blanket, stood up with my wet lap, and gave her a hug. She could see that I was overwhelmed by the magnitude and weight of the day. As we stood there tangled up in our hug, she whispered, "Don't turn around." Unlike my game of telephone with the nail technician days earlier, there was no mistaking her words. I had a tendency to get overwhelmed and overanalyze, even in grade school, so she must have known her words were sound advice. I thanked her and sat back down.

You know what happened next? Yup, I turned around. I moved my head slightly to the right pretending to scratch my chin on my shoulder. Real sly. I didn't swivel around enough to get the full picture, but I had a good idea of what was playing out behind us.

It was standing room only. All of the seats were filled, the back of the room was standing, and I could see people crammed into the entry area where I sat the day before for the family viewing and, days before that, picked out the casket.

How Much Love Is Possible in the World

Chase was on this Earth for a short time. He hadn't met a whole lot of people yet. I couldn't believe it. How had he reached so many? Were they here for him? Were they here for me and Marcus? I started to doubt my own worthiness. I was confused, overwhelmed, thankful, grateful and still sad. I wondered if Chase could see this. Did he feel this display of love? To this day, years and years later, I'll be talking to someone and they'll reference being at Chase's service. Trying not to look like a deer in headlights, I smile and immediately think to myself, "Wait, you were there?" It's probably the only party where I don't remember who attended and I can't blame it on an overserving of booze.

Our officiant for the service, Barbara, was the same wonderful woman who had married Marcus and me. She was composed, warm, gentle, and calming. She was everything we needed and that Chase deserved. She didn't get to meet Chase either but he would have liked her a lot too. Marcus and I decided not to speak at the funeral. I am a bit of a crier, even on a regular day. I wanted to speak about Chase, but I was so afraid that I wouldn't get it out. I needed so badly for people to hear about him if this was their only chance. They could watch me be a crying mess some other time. Literally any time at all. So Barbara read our words and she did it beautifully.

As children, we never stop thanking our parents for all that they give us. But today we want to thank you, Chase, for all that you've given us.

Thank you for showing us what handsome really looks like. You had the best features from the both of us: a perfect smile, beautiful big eyes, and soft dark hair. We wanted to pinch ourselves...how did we get so lucky?!

Thank you for teaching us real laughter. It took a couple of months to hear those magical sounds...but it was so worth the wait! Your laugh was perfect! It was infectious and taught us how to laugh in a whole new way.

Thank you for showing us how much love is possible in the world. The second you were born, we felt it. It was planted and has been growing and growing ever since. It will never go away and will always help us keep you close to our hearts.

67

Thank you for teaching us to dance. We read in all of the parenting books about making sure to have a bedtime routine...something to calm the baby as he gets ready to sleep. We couldn't think of anything better than having a dance party in the family room at 9:00 p.m.

Thank you for being part of our team. In some small (okay, maybe big) way, you knew you had to be a Dodgers fan, an A's fan, a Guns N' Roses singer, and a Cal Poly Mustang. Apparently we hadn't learned the lesson yet about how to not be too pushy.

Thank you for letting us smother you with kisses and hugs. The number "1" didn't exist when it came to those. They were always long and never-ending.

Thank you for making us morning people. One of the best times of the day was first thing in the morning. You'd wake up talking in the crib and playing with your hands. Sometimes we thought we were going to have to race each other to your room, to see who would get to you first.

To sum it up, thank you for being the most perfect son two parents could ask for. These past six months have been amazing and ones that will go down in history as the best—EVER!

We will always miss you, always think about you, always love you, and never forget you.

Love,
Your Mom & Dad

When we were planning the service the week before, we'd gone over the program, picked the casket, designated the pall-bearers, secured our plots, and finalized placement of the front yard porta potties. We'd even talked about the drive over to the cemetery after the service, for the graveside service. What I hadn't prepared myself for was physically getting from one place to the other. At least not with so many eyes watching. With so many family and friends I felt extremely supported, but I also felt on display.

Our immediate family was set to exit the little chapel through the front side door, closest to the hearse parked outside, and everyone else had been directed to leave the service out the back door from which they had arrived. My dad guided me to our door and pointed to their car waiting across the parking lot. Gripping Chase's now very sweaty blanket, I took a few steps outside. I slowly glanced to the right and there was...everybody. The sea of sad eyes staring at me. Okay, maybe that's a little conceited. I'm sure some of them weren't looking at me, but it sure as heck felt like it. I quickly ducked back into the mortuary. Panic was starting to creep in. I looked at my dad, shaking my head with fear. "I can't do this. I can't do this," I repeated. He probably knew it would only get harder the more time I was given to sit in my thoughts. Kinda like the time he dropped me off for tennis tryouts in high school and drove away before I had time to second-guess my abilities and jump back into a moving car.

With a gentle pep talk and before I had the chance to curl up in a ball on the chapel floor, he encouraged me to keep walking. I stepped out the door again and with laser focus and a pace that would make mall walkers jealous, I got to the car and quickly shut the door. I was safe again. Cheryl, my best friend, was supposed to drive with us to the cemetery. I had left her in the dust. Thankfully, we're still best friends. I'm grateful that she understood that I needed her, I just couldn't see her at that moment. She hitched a ride to the cemetery with someone else.

When we arrived at the cemetery, Chase's casket had already been placed over the spot we had picked for him. I was still happy with our choice of setting, but it just looked different seeing it now with the hole in the ground. The graveside service had a smaller crowd, but it was still a little overwhelming. I remember sitting there in front of the casket and hearing the sobs of someone behind me. After a little while curiosity got the best of me and I'd shaken that fear of turning around. I turned around to see that it was our cousin, Kelly. Her precious baby boy, Blake, had passed away less than a year earlier. She could cry all she wanted. So could everyone else, but her tears were different. I now understood they were the same as mine.

Wanting to Turn Around but Choosing to Face Forward

Once the graveside service was done Marcus and I continued to sit there. To my surprise, so did everyone else. No one was moving. The funeral director had come over in the hearse and approached Marcus and me. I looked at him and asked, "Now what do we do?" He informed us that etiquette is for others to stay in their places while the immediate family gets up to leave. I immediately hated etiquette. I wanted to stand up and let everyone know I wanted them to leave. Actually, *I wanted none of this.* I wanted a few more minutes with Chase. I mean, this would be it.

But I followed the stupid etiquette (remember, I'm a people-pleasing rule follower) and we got in the car. Here I was, leaving my son—again. Just as I had done the morning he died, when I got in my car to go to work. Except this time there would be no last kisses, last cuddles, last soft touch of his tiny pudgy baby knuckles. As we started to drive away, I turned around for one last look, like I had done with his car seat the day he died, and then faced forward. I feel like this is symbolic of life with grief—wanting to turn around, but knowing you have to face forward.

As I faced forward, I decided to set my focus on the after-party. No need to look too far ahead. It was safe to say this mom needed a drink. I somehow thought that once the service was over there would be this letdown and feeling of relief that it was over. Except this wasn't a wedding or a company Christmas party. The event was over but the dang feelings weren't going anywhere. The reality that Chase wasn't here still remained. I tried to play it all off once we got back to the house. Time to be a hostess. I offered people drinks, thanked them for coming, and tried my best to avoid the "f" word—funeral. No matter how many drinks I tried to consume, getting a good buzz was not in the cards that day. I was actually jealous of one of my friends for being drunker than I was. Looking back, it's probably a good thing it was her and not me.

There was quite a baby boom amongst my friends and me that year. I had told all the new moms that they were welcome to bring their babies with them if they were thinking about coming to Chase's service. They would be traveling hours to get here and I assured them it was okay. Less than two weeks earlier I had been that new mom and I now knew how painful it is to be apart from your baby. I know now I was just trying to assure myself it was okay. I was going to be okay.

Am I Cheating on Chase?

I was really trying to lean into the appearance of "everything's fine." In fact, I may have gone a little too far and tipped over into "everything's great" territory. That was definitely a stretch.

Partway through the afternoon my charade led me to make a horrible decision. I reached out and asked to hold my friend's baby boy. What better way to prove to people that I was a total champ by being not only near small children, but to physically be touching one?

The minute he was in my arms I wanted to drop him. If there had been an offer to start a game of baby hot potato I would have gladly joined in—and won. I felt nauseous, like I was doing something horrible. I felt like I was cheating on Chase. This little boy didn't feel right. He wasn't mine. He weighed different, moved differently, looked different, looked at me differently, and—most importantly—*where the heck was that feeling of joy when you hold a baby*? My heart, arms, and mind felt heavy and I wondered if maybe this is just what it is now. Or, after a few weeks, maybe I was just rusty. Either way, the whole thing was depressing.

I wondered what people around me were thinking at that moment. Were they proud of me for taking this step? Were they cringing in horror? Maybe they didn't even notice because, unlike me, they'd gotten that good buzz? I don't know how long this baby holding went on before I handed him back. Two minutes, ten minutes? It didn't matter because it was all too long. I don't care if I was just rusty. I wasn't getting back on this bike for a long time. I gently handed him back to his mom.

Surrounded by People but Alone

By late afternoon, after most people had gone home or back to their hotels, it was really quiet. Too quiet. With all of the busyness over the last several weeks, I was kinda enjoying not having enough space to think. Even just thinking about thinking was giving me anxiety.

Over the next few days, we were back to goodbyes. Our friends and family were heading back home, back to work, back to school, back to their lives. I didn't think it would be so hard to say goodbye, but I'd done too much of that recently and I was over it. As I said goodbye, what I really wanted to say was "please don't leave me." The tears that followed after every sendoff felt like it was a last goodbye all over again. At some point there would be no more goodbyes and everyone would just be gone.

Marcus and I weren't ready for that reality yet. So we decided to use the last days of our bereavement leave from work to take a trip, just the two of us. We'd spend a few days traveling up to Santa Cruz. I had fooled myself into thinking this trip was going to be like any other road trip we'd taken. You know—fun. I wanted so badly to believe that physically leaving our house was just as good as stepping away from life. I actually made a playlist for the car trip. In my defense, it was less "Pump Up the Jam" by Technotronics and more "Free Fallin'" by Tom Petty. Either way, a few songs and some tires to the pavement weren't helping me forget anything. Oh and Santa Cruz, our destination of choice, is forever ruined. I'm just thankful we hadn't picked Hawaii or some other dream destination. No offense to Santa Cruz. It wasn't you; it was me. Definitely me.

Santa Cruz is a seaside town nestled on the California coast. It has some nice beaches and an amusement park. Being that we had a complete lack of amusement, we skipped the park and stuck to our beachside inn. From our balcony I could still hear the screams coming from the park's roller coasters. These weren't the screams from roller coaster enthusiasts, but the ones from first timers who were utterly terrified and convinced they'd never make it off alive. It was as if my internal monologue had a voice. After a few days of drinking in a hotel room and having some sad seaside meals where we avoided eye contact with anything that resembled a person or a happy family, we drove down the coast to our next destination. Yes, I realize the complete irony of wanting to be around people but not actually wanting to be around people.

For our next spot, we rented a condo at a beachside resort. They had lots of amenities on-site so we didn't have to immerse ourselves amongst the crowds as much. We could sit on the beach and then grab a drink at the bar. And that's exactly what we did.

There was an access trail to the beach. We made our way down to the water where we sat watching the waves and talking. There was a family sitting nearby. In an odd twist of events, their joyous presence didn't bother me. While Marcus and I sat and talked about where we were going to go from here (not on this trip, but with life), the nearby family was digging holes in the sand.

Unexpectedly, their little girl made her way over to us. Marcus handed her a sand dollar. A pile of unbroken sand dollars had been left on the beach next to where we sat down. The little girl's family smiled back at us as their little bathing beauty waddled back over to start digging again.

As Marcus and I sat there talking about the weight and uncertainty of our pain, I believe we were purposefully interrupted by that little girl. It's almost like she could see our sadness (surprisingly, I wasn't actually crying) and wanted to remind us that there are still happy moments to be found for us. This wasn't the end. I carry this encouragement with me today and remind myself to stay open to seeing moments like this—when I feel like I was meant to cross paths with someone. When time seems to stand a little more still just for me. When

I see the white butterfly cross through the yard, and I happen to catch a glimpse. These moments aren't accidental. They are gifts, grown from my own story.

The Most Beautiful Bottle

It's totally cool if you think I'm a little wackadoo right now. I have these same thoughts sometimes. But some moments grown from grief are more "in your face" meant for you.

After the sand dollar exchange Marcus and I walked back up from the beach to the lounge/bar area of our resort. We found some stools at the bar counter and nestled in. We had nowhere else to be and I'm a sucker for people watching. We made small talk with the bartender and with a gentleman sitting next to us, who was there for a business trip. He didn't ask us why we were there—yet. We watched some drunk twenty-somethings hang on each other while trying to stay in tune with the music being played. Emphasis on *try*. Geez, I miss those simpler and off-key and off-tempo times.

As the man sitting next to us was getting ready to leave, he asked us what had brought us there. Poor guy, here we go. Marcus and I both paused, wondering who was going to take this one, and then we both kinda chimed in, with Marcus carrying the response to completion.

"We just buried our son and needed to get away for a few days."

"Oh, Jesus, I'm sorry," the businessman replied as he bought us our next round of drinks before closing his tab. In case you're wondering, a free drink is always a nice response.

As I was debating what my next drink would be, I looked behind the bartender to the long wall of liquor bottles. And there I saw it: a tall glass bottle with "Chase" written beautifully up the side. I asked the bartender about the bottle and he brought it over to me. Turns out there is a Chase distillery in England. Maybe that's not weird in and of itself. But how about that the universe threw me this fun fact at this exact moment? I'm going to steal this as another moment specially curated for me and brought to you by my very own tragedy, *thankyouverymuch*. If nothing else, it was a nice distraction while our life stayed in a waiting pattern.

Negative Infinity and the Rabbit Hole of Doubt

We were waiting to go back to our daily life and still waiting for answers on how Chase died, if they could come at all. After returning from Santa Cruz, we received Chase's preliminary autopsy results, with the official report arriving months later. We were sitting in our bed back at home, when Shari, from the coroner's office, called us. I'd summarize the conversation for you, but it's just as easy to share a snippet from the autopsy report itself. I must warn you that an autopsy is the most horrible read in the entire world. On a rating scale of one to ten, with one being awful, I'd give it a negative infinity rating.

> ### Closing Statement
> Based upon the investigation I ascribed the manner of death to be **<u>Natural</u>** and the cause of death to be **Cardiac Arrhythmia** (min) due to **Coarctation of Aorta** (congenital) with **Suspected Chromosomal Abnormality** as other significant condition contributing to death as determined by Forensic Pathologist Dr. B.H. I completed and signed the death certificate as the aforementioned manner and cause.

A congenital heart defect and a potential chromosomal abnormality. Natural. How incredibly specific and generic.

And, um, "Closing Statement"? I guess it's just too wordy to call it "The Statement That Will Never Capture the Wonder and Beauty of This Perfect Little Boy." You can keep "Closing Statement," doctor. I know the truth.

I had anticipated that these results would give me some sort of closure or, at the very least, would have guided me into a reasoning other than the world is just an extremely cruel place. It didn't. I started to ask myself questions. Why didn't I know? Should I have gone ahead with further testing after the genetic counseling appointment when I was pregnant? They had assured us that everything looked fine. Looking back, were there any signs? Should the hospital have picked up on these things when he was born? The pediatrician? Would the outcome have been different if those NICU nurses had taken Chase with them in those first moments after he was born? Bottom line, could we have saved him?

Chase had fair skin. He didn't poop every day. He was six months old and wasn't able to turn over on his own yet. In hindsight, maybe these were signs that something was wrong. Looking back, I believe these were signs. I just don't know. *I won't ever know.* Everyone saw his complexion. I'd brought up the lack of daily bowel movements to his pediatrician. Every child takes life at their own pace (heck, the same goes for adults)—he would turn over when he was ready. I'm not passing blame; I'm trying to say I shouldn't be so hard on myself when my mind goes to some pretty dark places.

Over the years I have had to become okay with "I don't know." What's my other option? I could have done more? He wasn't taken from me—I let him go. I failed him?

I gotta tell ya, that rabbit hole of doubt does not serve me or my sanity. My heart has become okay with "I don't know." It has turned into a true belief that he was meant to be our angel. It's no longer something I say to make myself feel better or deflect from the deeply saddening possibility of some other reason—for the most part, anyway.

I want you to believe it's not your fault, either, but you might not be there yet. It's not something you can just make happen with brute force and some elbow grease. Wouldn't that be nice? The things you're having to push out of the way are the thoughts that aren't serving you and those can be kind of elusive. Some days, the blame is right in front of you. Some days, it's circling around you, just loud enough to be distracting, but far enough away that you can't slap it out of the way. Some days, you're just really mean to yourself, and some days you actually see hints of self-kindness. There are days when the mind is quieter—those are the good days. Hold onto those. They are a reminder that you're doing it. You're opening yourself up to something other than blame. You don't need brute force because it's happening.

Some distraction never hurts either.

FIVE – HAVE YOU TALKED TO HR ABOUT THIS?

SUFFERING A LOSS DOESN'T come with a lot of rules. As well it shouldn't. Love is big, so grief is rightfully messy. However, being a functioning working adult often comes with lots of rules. There are things called employee handbooks and a department called Human Resources. This is not a dig on Human Resources—it's a hard job; there is no "Common Sense Handbook" we're all working from. When loss and grief collide with work, it's not exactly two puzzle pieces that fit easily together. If you're wanting to ensure you don't lose your job and source of income on top of it all, you might be asking yourself some questions: What's the right amount of mess I can bring with me every day? How much can I show I'm struggling before I get called into someone's office? How long am I "allowed" to not be fully present? How can I care about the bottom line when I'm at my own bottom? It's not just your own emotions you're working with either. Remember the lack of a "Common Sense Handbook?" It might have you asking questions like, "How long until so-and-so says something insensitive? Can I anticipate every comment that will come my way?

Marcus and I went back to work about two and a half weeks after Chase passed away.

I couldn't wait to get back to my day job of financial analysis, forecasting cash flows, and answering emails. The thought of sitting back at my desk where I received the news that Chase was gone sounded like a comforting place to be.

Yeah, totally being sarcastic. I didn't return to work so quickly because I missed work. I returned to work because I missed my home. The home that I was sitting in had become a little unrecognizable and less cocoon-ish with everyone gone now. So at least going to work had me staying in motion with a splash of familiarity.

Some might say two and a half weeks is really fast. Unfortunately, it's not uncommon for US corporate bereavement policies to provide employees with less than a week of time off for the loss of an immediate family member. If it seems like that's not enough time, well, it's because it isn't. It's not enough time to have a funeral, receive official autopsy results, and cry less frequently than every day. And how very kind of corporate America to offer the use of vacation hours if additional time is needed (but please check with your manager).

While these "rules" weren't on my side, my work friends and manager were. That's always the hope, I guess, and I was a fortunate employee. My relationship with my manager had already morphed into something a little more unconventional. He had become part of my story. He had driven me to see Chase for the last time. He saw me embrace Marcus in the middle of the street that day. He picked up my mom at the train station. Along with several other coworkers, he and his wife were at Chase's funeral. We had been in communication during those few weeks that I was not at work. Although he wasn't bothering me with much work at all, those brief calls with him gave me a sense of normalcy and a much-needed escape from the unknowing that the rest of my life had kicked up.

Scary Steps Forward

In preparation for my return to work, my office friends suggested a smaller department gathering a few days before I went back into the office. I was terrified to go back into the office. Not only was it where I received the worst news of my life, but the thought of feeling on display again, like I did at the funeral, would send my body into the early stages of a panic attack. All I could picture were people staring at me, feeling awkward around me, and not knowing what to say. I didn't know how I was going to navigate it all and I straight up didn't wanna! (Insert small tantrum with a foot stomp here.)

This smaller work get together would be less of a pre-party and more of a dry run. The goal was for me to feel like I had a larger team of support surrounding me while I navigated the larger scope of awkwardness that I'd be exposed to back in the office. Let me tell ya, there would be plenty to pick from.

There were about twenty of us and we all met at a local restaurant. I really liked the restaurant they had picked. Fun fact: it was also where I'd had Chase's baby shower with my closest family and friends about seven months earlier. I didn't have the heart to tell my coworkers this, and to be honest, while part of me wanted to never go back there, the other part of me thought it might make me feel closer to him. The restaurant had set us up in their side banquet room for more privacy and seating. Yup, the same room as the baby shower.

I'm not sure who benefited most from meeting up, me or my coworkers. Although the thoughts may have crossed my mind, I didn't crawl into the restaurant on my hands and knees and proceed to ugly cry over my nachos. My coworkers got to see that I was still me (on the outside anyway). I smiled like I hadn't seen my friends in a while. I think we all did our best to keep each other's spirits up, whatever that meant. It was a balancing act of acknowledging why we were all there, with a thorough dusting of avoidance.

When we were all done with our light appetizers and small talk and ready to leave, I walked out to the parking lot with a handful of ladies from the office. I'm not sure if it was because there were now fewer of us around, or maybe I'd been masking my level of "alrightness" a little too much again, but I chose that moment to really open up about my fears of returning to work and do that ugly crying thing I didn't want to do over the nachos a few hours earlier. They were all really kind and said that they would be there to help me through it. I knew they wanted to protect me as their friend, but I also knew that they couldn't keep me protected from everything. The truth of the matter is that this happened to me and not them. This was going to be my road to navigate and bumps were expected—and unavoidable.

I was scared about all these steps forward I was taking. Steps to the restaurant. Steps back into the office. Steps away from Marcus. Most of my days were still stuck in the emotions of wanting to hang on to the past. I mean, the past wasn't that long ago. Less than a month earlier I still had my son with me. Cracking a smile wasn't the hard part. Doesn't it technically take more muscles to frown? The hard part was finding a place to put all the junk that was happening underneath the smile. I'm sure a lot of what was going on emotionally played an important role in making room for a life of living with grief, but it also made me feel like a hoarder. Not a hoarder of physical tchotchkes but mental ones. My thoughts were getting a little crowded. Maybe this was all too much?

Overflowing Oatmeal and Emotions

This is a lot like when I heat up oatmeal in the microwave. I'm notorious for cooking things for way too long. About a minute passes and I watch the oatmeal start to fluff up and bubble a little. I'm pleased with how it's going, but then I get too confident. I decide to let it cook just a little bit longer and then I pick this specific moment to step away from the microwave for just a quick second. I return only to find oatmeal oozing out of the bowl and overflowing onto the spinning tray. I tell myself that I went too far. I pushed it just a little too much. The next time I won't let it go on for so long.

What I'm trying to say here is that I'm a bowl of oatmeal. What I'm also trying to say is that maybe I was pushing myself too much. Maybe. But at the same time, I knew I had to keep trying. As long as I kept trying, one of these times maybe the emotions would be less and the weight of every task would be less. At some point I wouldn't run the risk of messily spilling over onto the moving tray of life all the time. I just had to take it all minute by minute—literally so on many days.

Marcus and I left each other that first morning of work with the hope that the day would be over soon and we'd be back together. We reminded each other that we were just a phone call away if we needed to talk. It felt horrible to leave each other and neither of us wanted to do it.

I walked quietly into the office. I rounded the corner to my cubicle. I was relieved that my coworkers had taken down some of the pictures I'd asked them to from my small fuzzy walls, like Chase's birth announcement and other happy baby things. I had been pregnant at the same time as my coworker who sat in the cubicle across from me. We'd had a joint work baby shower, and Chase and her son were less than a month apart. Remember my hatchback collision with the garage? I had actually been on the way to her house for that playdate that day. I noticed that she had taken down her son's pictures from my line of sight. She didn't have to do that. I didn't want others to feel like they had to hide their happiness because my world was sad (okay, the "mean" part of me did), but I gladly welcomed muted enthusiasm. I knew I couldn't expect that convenience all the time. Others still had their kids' finger paintings proudly displayed. I resisted the urge to rip them down.

Beautiful Gifts

Someone had placed a card on my keyboard. I nervously opened it, unsure of what sentiment it would hold. It was from one of my pregnant coworkers. We had been sharing in this recent wave of the office baby boom.

Her card explained that she was worried about how seeing her baby bump would make me feel and she wanted to be sensitive to what I was going through. She didn't want to do or say the wrong thing and she wanted to give me any and all of the space I needed. This was a beautiful gift. When someone is going through a hard time I've often asked myself, "How do I tell them I don't want to say the wrong thing, without saying the wrong thing?" Well, the answer, as an example, is a card like hers.

I didn't feel ignored. *I felt acknowledged.*

I didn't feel uncomfortable. *I felt validated.*

I didn't feel angry. *I felt cared about.*

I messaged this mom over the company's computer chat, to thank her for her kindness. I'd have to work up to an in-person meeting where I actually walked over to her office and acknowledged her bump with the smiles that it deserved. Thankfully, because of her card, I knew that was okay with her. I'd probably end up running into her on a random walk to the bathroom anyway but I didn't feel the need to be an overachiever. She had relieved the pressure.

Believe it or not, there were moments when I actually did try to work. One day I was in my manager's office with a few people when I had my first conversation with someone outside of my department. It was our company's CEO at the time.

"It's great to see you," he said with a soft smile. It wasn't overly enthusiastic, but it wasn't paired with sad eyes either. I wondered if he'd practiced. You're right, probably not.

I had prepared myself for a lot more dialogue during these first encounters with people (as the "new me"). So as the words were coming out of his mouth I was inhaling like someone would as they're preparing to make the world's longest acceptance speech for the best actor nod at the Academy Awards. The really awkward kind of speech where the orchestra starts to play over them right about the time the actor is thanking Jesus. As hard as it may be for you to believe that I'd drone on awkwardly, I was prepared for that extremely rare chance. Except I'm going to rip this band-aid off right now. In the early years of grief, I wasn't in the mood to thank Jesus. Spoiler alert: it'll never be a "thank you," but I do feel His presence again in a capacity that's just right for me.

In this pleasant turn of events, the prolonged dialogue didn't need to happen. So, in an effort to avoid sounding like a balloon losing all its air in a flapping and mighty force, I could feel myself slowly exhale the overestimated breath in. Then, the few of us who were still standing together in that office resumed our work, staring at numbers on a spreadsheet. To give the others credit, they were actually analyzing the numbers. I was probably the only one literally just staring at them. If life wasn't making sense, what was the point of a spreadsheet?

But there you have it. That was my favorite conversation when I came back to work. No mention of dying, loss, babies, an awkward hug, forced small talk, or what would have been the worst—an exchange with absolutely no substance because the other person had preemptively decided we were going to pretend like nothing happened.

My interaction with the CEO wasn't an open-ended question with an obvious answer like "How are you doing?" (I know, most of the time it just comes out.) Rather, it was simply nice to see me. A statement that conveyed, "Hey, you're going through something really awful, and I just want to say it's nice to see your face around here again. Now get back to work." Okay, I'm totally kidding about that last part, but it is nice to feel like a valuable contributor. You want to know the best part of this short exchange? It didn't warrant any more effort from me than a "thank you"—and even then, probably only if I felt like it. How we interpret conversations can be pretty subjective, but for me, this was a great one.

Lessons in Avoidance Techniques

It was a short walk from my manager's office to my desk. Believe it or not, I actually did feel safe hiding behind my cubicle walls. I initially thought my desk would be the hardest place to be. But the thought of venturing out into the further reaching communal areas, like the kitchen, where I could bump into absolutely anyone, was terrifying. This building that I'd been coming to five days a week for three years suddenly felt like a field of landmines. I had to be more strategic and careful about where I was stepping.

I did eventually make it to the kitchen. I was getting thirsty and damn you, water, for being a necessity. I stood up from my desk and I could see from across the room that the kitchen lights were off. I was taking that as a potentially good sign that no one had triggered the motion sensors and the place would be empty. No such luck. I gave the wall light switch the stink-eye as I walked in and saw a coworker quietly standing at the sink. I asked how she was. I felt immediate regret. Why must I always feel the need to break the silence? Truth be told, I was just gearing up for when she'd ask me the same question in return. She didn't. Phew. Instead, I spent several minutes hearing about the recent birth of her new grandson. Ummmmm...

Operation "Get the Heck Back to My Desk Now" had officially commenced. I didn't want to cut her off, because that would be rude. Yes, I realize the potential irony here, but I know her heart was in the right place. So I listened, smiling politely, and then went back to my cubicle safe space. She knew about Chase, so I interpreted her choice of conversation topic as a way to help me avoid my sadness. A fruitless endeavor. As if I were thinking, "Thank you so much for talking about the new baby in your life. For a few minutes there I was able to completely forget about burying mine."

I did my best to avoid future casual conversations using some specific techniques:

Walk with a purpose.

Pretend you didn't see them.

Use "I didn't see ya there" when conversation becomes unavoidable.

Show up to conference rooms with seconds to spare, demonstrating my new mantra of "Late is Great!"

Bury myself in my computer and blame my lack of interaction on deadlines.

If all else fails, hide out in a bathroom stall for a few minutes (maybe a few hours, tops).

I guess I could have put up a sign around my neck that said "please leave me alone," but that seemed like too simple of a plan and Human Resources would probably frown upon that, even with the word "please." Spoilsports.

While I had my strategies laid out for trying to avoid conversation, I was less skilled in the art of escaping a conversation that had already started. I feel like I've always struggled with this, so I'm not sure I could blame this entirely on the present circumstances.

Once, I was wrapping up in a meeting when one of the attendees asked if he could talk to me for a second. I assumed it was about something related to the meeting we had just had. Instead, he started to tell me about his idea for a crib mattress. The mattress would be able to signal to parents when a child was in distress while sleeping. I can't remember the exact specifics of the invention and I didn't have the heart to tell him that products like this already existed. His idea would probably capture 5 percent of the market share at best. What he wanted to know from me is if I thought something like this would be helpful. What he was really asking me was if I thought his mattress invention could have helped save my son.

What would have been most helpful is to not have this conversation. I didn't have my child to protect anymore and hypotheticals built after the death of a loved one are not constructive— and that's putting it mildly and in the most polite manner I know how. I did decide to tell him that there were products like this already in existence and yes, I'm sure they're very helpful, generally speaking. Then, I quickly grabbed my computer and pretended to be late for my next (pretend) meeting. I was way nicer than that *Shark Tank* panel would have been. Maybe I shouldn't have been.

Not all my office interactions were one-on-one. With larger companies, unfortunately group events are a thing. My company held a series of annual summer barbecues. Some of the musically inclined employees would perform in the parking lot, while others cooked on an open grill. My contributions to these events consisted of listening and eating. One of these summer barbecues happened shortly after I returned to work. That day coworkers kept encouraging me to go downstairs with them and get some food. In hindsight, it would have been safer to be surrounded by my support team. Instead, I assured them I'd be down shortly as I pretended to be up against one of those conversation-avoiding deadlines I mentioned earlier.

Eventually I did get hungry and brave enough to get food. I believed I could handle it. It's not like I had to be the one to start the dance floor or anything. Just grab a plate and some barbecue. As I walked outside and entered the food line, I was immediately overwhelmed. There were so many people. The music was playing and there was *lots* of talking. As I stood there, in what I hoped was the back of the food line, I tried to put on a smile like I wanted to be there. In reality, everything in me wanted to run. I quickly realized that I hadn't seen or talked to a lot of people since I'd come back to work, and I was way more vulnerable and exposed than I needed to be.

If you haven't noticed, I'm not a big fan of the "open concept" work environment. To my relief, no one tried to talk to me. I believe I have the awkwardness of grief to thank for that. There wasn't a race to run up to the newly bereaved mom and ask how summer was going. I wouldn't have if I were in their shoes. By the time I got up to the front of the line, my level of overwhelm had peaked, and I'd made up my mind that I would just throw some food on my plate and get the heck back inside. You know, those darn "deadlines" again. With my plate of food in hand, I rushed inside the building and back up the stairs—not caring if I dropped a chicken wing on the way. I sat quickly back in my cubicle listening to the muffled sound of the band from one story above. I was relieved to be by myself again. Embracing my loneliness.

Some Days I Left Early via the Back Staircase

When I talk about embracing my loneliness, I'm talking about the time when you feel slightly swept out to sea. You're not so far out that you can't see the shore (the hopeless moments), but you're far out enough that over the waves, you still catch the view of people having fun on shore. You're just not quite sure how or when you'll want to get back there. If you fight the current and try too hard to swim, it'll make it worse and the last thing you want to feel, or revisit, is panic. So you tread water and stay where you are, in the loneliness. At some point the water doesn't feel as cold as when you first fell in, so you decide to comfortably stay where you are. The happy screams from shore still seem like a bit too much anyway. Sooner or later, when currents start to shift, you'll notice yourself naturally drifting closer to shore. It won't happen with one resolving and overwhelming wave, but more like lots of helpful ripples.

I wondered how long I'd be treading water and embracing my loneliness. Not just on company barbecue day, but in the days to come. There was a time not long ago that I enjoyed being part of the crowd, whether it was the lunchtime barbecues or talking with other new moms about baby feeding schedules. Now, things were different.

With the recent office baby boom, it wasn't uncommon to

have cute little diaper-clad visitors in the office. Proud working parents shared their newest family members with the people they spent most of their days with. Coworkers enjoyed the work reprieve for baby show-and-tell. Chase and I had stopped by the office a few months prior when I was still on maternity leave. It was almost a rite of passage. So I knew it would happen again at some point. When it did, maybe it was the element of surprise that got me? Who knows, but it sucked.

The echoing baby cry could be heard over the sound of loud typing. There was a universal deep breath in from the cubicle crowd as we were all a little startled by the sudden sound. Part of me wondered for a brief second which one of my coworkers was having a meltdown. I wouldn't judge—adulting is hard. Then came the group "awww" and whispers as everyone realized it was actually a baby's cry. People began hypothesizing about whose baby was here to visit.

Some ladies stood up immediately trying to look over the sea of cubicle walls to find where the noise was coming from. They quickly started their voyage toward the sound, dodging mini trash cans in the hallway and calculating the fewest steps needed to get to a straightaway. Not me. I stayed cemented to my chair.

That initial baby cry felt like a gut punch. For a minute I felt like I was daydreaming about when tending to that cry used to be *my* job. My favorite job. My stomach flipped a little, wondering if my daydream was so real that I was hearing Chase again. Then I received the wave of intense sadness knowing that I wasn't hearing him at all. I wanted to stay in my chair, but I also felt like grief was physically pushing me down. It felt so *heavy*.

"Are you coming?" someone asked. "I think that's Sarah's baby." I shook my head no, but I'm not sure if they saw because they'd already started walking toward the sound.

I didn't care whose baby it was. I wasn't going. In fact, I wanted to be going—out the door, into my car, back home, and into my bed. That sequence of events actually happened on a few occasions. On those days, I quietly packed up my things and exited the building down the back staircase. It was either excuse myself or let out a cry louder than any of those visiting office babies and immediately take the title for the world's worst (or best) office meltdown. I felt like I'd already stolen a lot of emotional thunder between these walls. Plus, my manager gave me the gift to "do what I needed to do." Kudos to me for being a reliable employee? So, with an overarching green light, "peace out" also became a frequent mantra.

While going back to work had thrown me back into something busy, it had pulled me away from something else. Someone else—Marcus. We were each other's safe place. So for those hours that we were apart every day, pretending, it felt like I was drifting out to sea. Pretending to work, pretending to care, pretending to be doing okay.

I always wondered how Marcus was doing. I wondered if people were being kind. I wondered if he was struggling with the same things I was. When we got home every day, these were the questions that came up. It wasn't quite as simple as "How was your day?"

For about a month, we'd get home, change clothes, mix some stiff drinks, and meet on the back patio for happy hour. Okay, "happy hour" is a little misleading, but I don't think anyone's coined a better phrase to encapsulate an hour of raw conversation about life's horrible struggles. Actually, I think it's called "therapy." Ours was a little different because it didn't include the copay and fear of judgment, but did include an added splash (heavy pour) of rum or vodka.

The Empathy Superpower

I was very lucky to have such a supportive community at work. I not only had my own feelings as validation, but I had something to compare to. Marcus's reentry to the workplace was not good. I wasn't there to witness it firsthand, but as his biggest fan, it was painful for me to see his struggle as he'd talk about his days. Upon hearing the stories, it wasn't unusual for me to say things like "I'm gonna march right down there..." or "Oh, I'll tell you what I'm gonna do...." I never acted on any of it, but I have to say, when I daydream about it even to this day, I'm commanding, articulate, and a force to be reckoned with. But I know that no matter how hard my bark or bite may be, nothing would change—because empathy is a skill to be learned for those who are open to it. Marcus's manager did not have empathy. In fact, he repelled it.

While my coworkers had donated weeks and weeks of paid time off to me (which I didn't take), his manager couldn't "make any guarantees" if Marcus needed some more time. Or when Marcus did take the time "offered," he was worried it would impact his job negatively.

Marcus worked at a brick and mortar store. I had the comfort of my cubicle and he was exposed to "the public." One day a customer came into the store with his young son. Marcus was helping the customer but struggling to stay focused as the sadness of seeing this man with his son was getting to be too much. His coworker—a true heroine—could see he was struggling and she stepped in to take over. Not all situations were bad, but when you're trying to hold onto hope and shake off the hurt at the same time, something is going to give. Like your emotional well-being. It means absolutely everything to feel supported by your manager and your work community.

Empathy is more than a skill. It's a learned superpower that should be celebrated and even rewarded. So I say give it a try, and if it feels like something you could do on a regular basis, slap that sucker on your resume. "I see that you're proficient in Microsoft Office and well versed in managing multiple SaaS systems. That's nice and all, but I'm more interested in the fact that you're always open to supporting coworkers when they're going through hard times. You sound like a wonderful human being. You're hired." Okay, I don't know if that's how it would go, but it sounds nice, right?

Empathy is trying to find understanding through someone else's experiences. You don't have to know what someone else is going through, but you're there for them while they are going through it. It's not something you just have or don't have. You have to practice. You have to be afraid to mess up. You have to want to be better.

Is empathy a skill that companies encourage their employees and management to nurture? Not really. Not directly, anyway. Should they? *Heck yeah!* I may be talking crazy now, but showing someone you care about them just might be the best benefit you can offer. I mean it definitely helps if it's stacked on top of a generous 401k matching program, but I'm more likely to stay at a company and contribute to the greater good (aka company's bottom line) if I feel genuinely cared about. It just might be the reason I've chosen to stay at the same company all these years and my husband has switched careers entirely (don't worry, I'll explain later).

To the manager who feels like their employee is "distracted" by grief, here's something to keep in mind: yes, you might have to meet your employee where they are at, at least for a little while. That short time of one person's reduced output and a larger team's show of humanity builds strength for the long term. It's the most encouraging thing you can do. Plus, it feels really good to be a kind human when someone is going through a tough time.

Escalators or Double Dutch

Navigating the early stages of grief is kinda like getting on an escalator. At least for those of us who are apprehensive and not too sure footed to begin with. Maybe for the more nimble it's like jumping into a game of Double Dutch? Let's focus on the escalator for now.

You stand at the foot of the escalator, preparing to hold onto the railing and try to time your first step onto the moving steps. Inevitably, someone whizzes by you on your left and they practically leap past you. You use their rushed energy as a sign that you need to get movin', or at the very least, show people (but mainly yourself) that you can do this. You hoist yourself onto a step and your hand clenches the railing for balance. You've got that first foot planted, but you've kinda forgotten about the other one. It hangs there for a minute, not sure exactly where to touch down. You notice that the step behind you is available, so you quickly grab it before someone else takes up the nearby real estate. At this point you ease your grip on the railing, just a little, and breathe a sigh of relief. You've made it on board. You slowly look up and see pedestrians who are actually walking on the escalator. I mean, really, people...motion on top of motion? A bit of overkill if you ask me. The ground is moving underneath you and you're holding on. That's enough of a win.

And just like with those early stages of grief:

You've immersed yourself back in the crowd.

You're moving with minimal effort, aside from the huge first step.

To those around you, it might actually seem like you know where you want to go.

In reality, you're just picking the path of least resistance because you can't do anything else but hold on to the railing and try to blend in.

So, to the manager: it shouldn't always be about how quickly you want someone to get on board or get back to work. It's meeting them at their pace *just for a bit*. Give them a sign so they know you're not going to just whizz by them on the left.

If you're feeling overwhelming personal loss coupled with the pressure to keep moving—whether as an employee or a human being—getting on that escalator gets easier every time you do it. So does living with grief. Don't force yourself to pole vault onto the escalator.

And if your work—or others—can't handle that, well, "I'm going to march right down there...!" I'm kidding (for the most part).

SIX – PREGNANCY FOR THE EMOTIONALLY UNSTABLE

I N THE MONTHS AFTER Chase died, in between work and our unhappy happy hours, Marcus and I attended grief counseling. That's right, I didn't become this emotionally stable on my own. Our counselor was the absolute best.

We were fortunate that our grief counselor also had a son who passed away. I know that "fortunate" may sound bad here, but as someone who's a big fan of therapy (my early twenties also had some really dark moments), feeling like the mental health professional sitting across from you just "gets you" is a gift.

When we met in her office for the first session, I immediately felt protected as we sank into the love seat of the dimly lit room. I didn't have to explain what it feels like to have your child die. I didn't feel pressure to make conversations comfortable for her. Or feel like I had to prove the depth of my pain to somehow justify that I was in the right place. She knew. And I clung to her wisdom of navigating painfully forward.

During that first visit, I could see the hurt as she shared about the loss of her own little boy. Her eyes welled up but she was composed. In an unsurprising turn of events, I started to ugly cry almost immediately. I cried because I was so sad for her. I was sad that I now knew the same pain. I cried because I was quickly realizing that this wasn't going to just go away. She had been carrying the loss of her son for a lot longer than me and it still had the strength to bring water to her eyes within moments. Being there with her was helpful, but as much as I'd hoped it would be, I quickly realized it wasn't a solution. I wasn't there to get past anything. I was simply getting pointers about how to carry it all with me.

Her tears also reassured me that I was in a safe place. I wasn't going to get emotionless textbook answers about coping skills. Or, if I did, at least they'd be masked by real life examples I could relate to, from someone who has been there. From someone who is still there. Still here. Marcus and I went to her office every week for several months. From July (after the funeral) and leading up to those first dreaded holidays. We talked about wanting to have more kids and how nervous we were about the upcoming holidays. Our counselor didn't have another child after her son died, so I was nervous to bring up the idea of having more children. I didn't want to be insensitive. I'd later recognize those nervous feelings as empathy. She was so understanding when I finally broached the subject and she gave us helpful insights.

She pointed out that even if I were to get pregnant again, it wouldn't stop the grieving. I'd be in the trenches (my words, not hers) whether I had a growing belly or not. I suppose that's how life is. Most of the time there's not a perfect starting point or finish line. It all kinda meshes together. And it's messy. So the decision was still ours—to try or not to try. Everything else was out of our hands. The only thing we were certain of was that if we waited for the grief to be over, Marcus and I would never have more kids. Because grief is never over.

First Beginnings

Chase wasn't the first time I was grieving the loss of a baby. In fact, he's my first rainbow baby, before I'd learned the term. I was pregnant almost two years before Chase was born. I went to my eleven-week appointment and laid on the crinkly papered exam chair, while Marcus watched the nurse try to find a heartbeat on the monitor. It never came. We had already told some of my close girlfriends and our immediate family about the pregnancy. Our due date would have been the week before Thanksgiving. We had started calling my bump "our little turkey."

The doctor was surprised that my body hadn't miscarried on its own by eleven weeks. Based on the size, he estimated that the baby had stopped growing about three weeks earlier (right after my last ultrasound). We scheduled a D&C for the following week. I had a follow-up appointment after the procedure.

We were told that it had been a partial molar pregnancy. I know—a what? Some sites on the internet kindly call it a "genetic accident." High level, there are too many chromosomes. In addition, there is a potential for complications after this type of pregnancy, so the doctor dropped some more bad news. He didn't want me to get pregnant for another year and I would be taking monthly blood tests to ensure my HCG levels stayed low. I gotta say, I've had better follow-ups.

Marcus and I tried to stay positive. This was just a little setback. We told ourselves that miscarriages are common. I'd call this a valiant effort at trying to suppress our grief. While statistically that may be true, it didn't, nor should it, dictate our feelings. If you fall off a bike and obtain a serious case of road rash, the last thing you'd want to hear as you're picking rocks out of open wounds is that you should shake it off—because this happens to everyone. Fun facts don't make the raw flesh throb any less, so just don't. Marcus and I were a bit of a mess when Thanksgiving rolled around. It should have been our due date. We should be a family of three. Instead we were day drinking and playing video games. We weren't grieving together. We got into an argument. As Marcus remembers it, I said some not so nice things. He's probably right.

This may be the unpopular opinion but, I believe, looking back, that our struggle to grieve together during that year of our miscarriage was meant to prepare us for losing Chase.

Intermission

Yup, one of these again—because we can. Just how I felt the hesitation talking to our grief counselor about trying again to have another baby, I feel that same hesitation talking about it with you. I want to at least give you a chance to pause first. If the thought of reading about me getting pregnant again gives you a sudden urge to light these pages on fire, then please wait to read ahead. Also, please put down the fire starter. I'd love to wrap you in a weird side hug and usher you forward, but that would be selfish—and slightly creepy. This book is for you to take at your own pace, so I respect where you're at. If you're still in bed at 1:00 p.m. on a Tuesday, trying to remember when you took your last shower, I feel you. I'll be here when you're ready to put your feet back on the floor. Also, I don't know if this helps at all, but spoiler alert, these upcoming pages still don't have me figuring it all out. If that wasn't teaser enough, continue when you're ready.

New Beginnings

I got pregnant with Bree in August, a few months after Chase died. Some people might think this is too soon. That's okay. That's an opinion and we're all allowed to have those. You're also allowed to keep that opinion to yourself (wink wink).

If you've ever read one of those expectant mother books, there are several "bad chapters." These are the chapters that address any concerns you might be having or helpful ways to identify if something isn't going as it should. These are the chapters you don't initially read because you're remaining positive that having a baby won't be hard for you. Well, I'd covered a few of those "bad chapter" topics already: miscarriage, partial molar pregnancy, infant death, and soon-to-be high-risk pregnancy. Safe to say there was no how-to guide for growing our family anymore, at least not the kind I was looking for. I didn't want a book about how blissful pregnancy is, unless I was starting a campfire and needed kindling. I wanted a book that celebrated anxiety and embraced a certain air of negativity. In the realm of growing our family we were writing our own book at this point and it had some serious feelings to it.

Being pregnant after child loss is not easy.

I'm really tempted to use the word "horrible" here, but it would only be to describe my emotional well-being and I'm trying to stave off too much outside judgment. I am so grateful, but the emotional insanity that was going on in my head was not healthy. This was the hardest time of my life. There were no irrational fears. There were just fears...validated possibilities that this wasn't going to end well.

When I was pregnant with Chase I was so happy. I was happy that I was going to be a mom.

When I was pregnant with Chase I loved the attention of my growing belly.

When I was pregnant with Chase I enjoyed talking with other moms.

When I was pregnant with Chase I couldn't wait to meet him.

When I was pregnant with Chase's siblings I was cautiously optimistic (on a good day).

When I was pregnant with Chase's siblings I didn't want anyone to acknowledge my growing belly.

When I was pregnant with Chase's siblings I didn't want to talk to other moms.

When I was pregnant with Chase's siblings I was perfectly okay with waiting to meet them in this world.

There are all these statistics about the risk of miscarriage during the first trimester. This leads some expectant parents to wait to share their baby news until the second trimester. When it's a "safer time." So, when was my "safer time"?

I knew what it felt like to tell friends and family "too early" that I was pregnant, only to have to tell them I had a miscarriage. I knew what it felt like to lie to coworkers about what I was doing that Friday I requested off from work to go in for my D&C. "Do you have something fun planned for the long weekend?" Not exactly.

Now I also knew what it felt like to stand over my son's casket. There was no "safer time" anymore. I could have really used a more precise statistic than "after the first trimester." I was thinking more along the lines of sharing the news *a lot* later.

Maybe something more like "Oh, I didn't tell you? Yeah, I had a baby and she's starting college next week." All this to say, I was feeling a little bit on an island now, so in layman's terms I'd be following the path of "winging it." This wasn't a route of pure chaos. It was more about letting my heart lead, with a healthy dose of going with my gut. Where are the expectant parenting books with that advice? Bueller? Bueller? This book is officially part memoir and part *What to Expect When You're Rightfully Terrified of Expecting.*

My initial theory was that as long as I kept the news to myself, I'd only have to worry about my own emotions. I wouldn't be subject to other people's opinions and I wouldn't feel like I was carrying around the weight of other people's worries as well as my own. I don't do nearly enough squats to condition myself to carry that heavy of a load.

On the other hand, the thought of telling people had me feeling indifferent. It was more of a "why not" attitude, rather than actually looking forward to sharing this joyous news with others. Everyone had already seen me at my worst (at least I'd hoped), so it didn't seem like I really had anything to hide.

Awkward Announcements

Ah, pregnancy announcements. They can be so much fun. Until they're not.

I remember telling my parents the news that I was pregnant after Chase died. We were in Monterey for my college room-mate's wedding. I was a bridesmaid. I knew friends would know something was up when I wasn't drinking. It's not that I'm a total boozehound, but it's a well-known fact that I think wine is delicious, especially when paired with an impromptu dance floor and an epic DJ.

Marcus and I went to my parents' hotel room before the wedding started. This didn't have the same feels as the viral videos on social media today. There were no streamers or surprise onesies for the grandparents to discover. It was actually pretty quiet. Marcus and I were quiet when we told them. We knew it would be a lot to unpack, because we were still unpacking the news for ourselves. I think they were trying to read the room at the same time they were processing their own emotions. It's not that we all weren't happy, but we didn't want to be overly happy in case that's not what someone else was looking for in the moment.

I could see it all in my parents' eyes—the joy and the fear. I think there was fear for a healthy pregnancy but also a parent's fear of not being able to protect us from the unknown (again). I would see that same joy and fear every time I told people I was pregnant. Or maybe they were just mirroring my own emotions. Either way, I saw it. I could see the fear and literally hear it. It came in the form of a big inhale before I heard the happy "Congratulations!" It was the inhale that sounded like, "Sweet Jesus, please let everything be okay for them this time." Except no one wanted to say that part out loud. Everyone wanted to tell me that it would all just be okay. I let them say it. I mean, it's not like I could stop them, but I knew the truth: nothing was guaranteed.

I could also sense the underlying sighs of relief. Like, "Oh, thank goodness they're moving forward." This only fueled my growing fear that people would forget about Chase. What if they started focusing forward at a pace way faster than what I was ready for? I didn't want to feel pressured to meet them up ahead. Remember the escalator? I didn't need to walk on the escalator to get anywhere at a faster speed than I was already traveling. I didn't want to feel like people had moved on and were speeding past me while quickly shouting, "On your left!" I was still thinking about Chase *every minute of every day*.

Can we just get comfortable with the idea that meeting someone where they are, with an empathetic "you're right, sometimes things just aren't okay" can be a common courtesy? Sure, sometimes you're like Princess Jasmine from Disney's *Aladdin*, enjoying the view from the magic carpet ride, but let's just acknowledge the fact that sometimes the magic carpet slips right out from underneath you and you realize that not everything is "shining, shimmering, splendid." Not being okay doesn't mean you're a total fun sucker. It doesn't mean you're destined for a life of forever depression (you're not). You're just moving through some serious poop. For other people to not acknowledge this—*they're* the weird ones! I spent nine months hoping that this time I could keep my baby. I also spent nine months preparing myself in case there had to be another goodbye. Yup—serious poop. I didn't need positivity. I needed understanding.

Emotional instability wasn't my only new takeaway with being pregnant again. I broke up with my previous OB-GYN, the one who skipped out on my delivery for a chance at Broadway (okay, *allegedly*). This wasn't a "it's not you, it's me" break-up. It was definitely all him. I never heard from him after Chase passed away. He knew what had happened because his interview was documented on the autopsy report. I called his office in the months after Chase died, because I had some questions related to some genetic testing I was researching. I talked to one of the nurses whom I'd seen there numerous times over the years. When I told her who I was, her voice became quiet. She said she was sorry to hear about what had happened, but she didn't put me on hold to grab the doctor or ask if I wanted to talk to him. I felt like I was being stopped at the gate and wasn't allowed in. I never heard from him again, despite all we'd been through. I wondered that if I wasn't "kind of a big deal" around that office, then who would be? I couldn't go back there.

I enlisted the help of a high-risk doctor. During my first visit to my new (and wonderful) OB-GYN, she asked how I was feeling. In hindsight, she may have just been asking about my vagina, but I took it as permission to start sobbing about my shaky mental state. So much for keeping it together. With her specialty field, I told myself that she's probably seen this type of hot mess plenty of times before. I actually found the subtle look of "here we go again" as comfort, as she washed her hands and grabbed a paper towel and a Kleenex for me without missing a beat. I was someplace where other worried moms had come before me and paved the way. Why not show the tears? I might as well be honest from the get-go about what she was workin' with. Also, if I'm going the defensive route, she should have known not to ask any form of the question "How are you doing?"

I enjoyed the honesty of these appointments, because it's somewhat of an odd concept to think that when you see some-one who's pregnant they could actually be sad and not want to talk about it. I used to ask expectant moms questions or share personal stories to try and connect with them using our common motherhood bond. Now I keep my mouth shut and give pregnant women a crooked smile on the off chance they're part of my new moms group and they don't want to talk about it. They'll still have plenty of opportunities for small talk with other people. I'll be the one who gives nods and fist bumps as if to say, "I've got you. We don't have to talk about it." I wish I'd received more fist bumps.

Cantaloupes and Grocery Delivery

Once, when I was about six months pregnant, I would have certainly preferred a quiet fist bump. I was in the produce section of the grocery store. It was my final stop before heading to the checkout line. I was focused on getting those last few items when I looked over and saw a very sweet-looking lady. She had short gray hair and thick glasses, and I could see her generous smile peeking out over the top of the pile of cantaloupes. She was smiling at me. You know that feeling when someone is about to strike up a conversation? They're looking at you with intention while they're still forming their opening sentence. I knew the small talk was coming but I didn't have the heart to say, "Let's not do this, okay?" What kind of mean girl shuts down a conversation before it's even started? Especially with a sweet old lady over cantaloupes? Cantaloupes are delicious. Life had me feeling a little robbed, but I didn't want to necessarily steal all the joy from other people either (okay, maybe a little bit on my particularly angry days).

The smile parted and she asked when I was due. Here we go.

I told her I had about three months left. Her smile got bigger thinking about how exciting of a time this must be for me.

She asked if I knew what I was having. I told her it was a little girl. Then it happened.

"Is this your first?" Ugh. A once simple mathematical question was now a choose-your-own- adventure story.

I could say a lot of things here:

No.

No, this is my second (child).

No, this is my third (pregnancy).

No, I have a son.

No, I have a son, but he died.

No, she has a big brother in Heaven.

Yes. (I mean, lying is an option)

I was always trying to weigh how I was feeling in the situation, which would inevitably lead to an awkwardly long pause on my part. What answer would speak to my heart in the moment and how was I feeling about the person I was talking to? Did I want to share or was my mission to keep this as short as possible? Did I want to flash my awkward grief card, or fit in with societal norms? So I replied:

"No, this is my second."

She asked if my first was a boy or girl.

"A boy."

"How perfect! A boy and a girl!" Then came the anecdotes about how busy I was going to be with two young ones. I just kept smiling. About this time I was really hoping she'd finish picking out her melons and shuffle to the register. Any other questions and I felt like my decision to keep it breezy would start to waver and I'd lean toward "let's see how uncomfortable this can really get." Sometimes the more I'd try to fit in with societal norms the angrier I'd get. Sure, I could have picked another answer upfront, but that would have just gotten me here faster. I've tried them all—except "yes." I'm a horrible liar.

If I include Chase in my response to "how many kids do you have?" I feel the comfort of talking about him and the conviction of love as his mom. I also feel the pain as I'm talking about my son whom I can't ever fully share. He's not beside me. I can't put my arms around him as I mention his name. No one will ever see the full joy that his life brought to this world, because they'll see some piece of my grief mixed in. That will always make me sad.

The moral of the story is this: say what feels right for you in the moment. The same answer doesn't have to apply all the time. The other lesson from this story is: start using grocery delivery services on particularly rough days so you can avoid the produce section altogether.

Already Madly in Love with Bree

I tried as much as possible to avoid situations that made days rougher than they needed to be. Sometimes I unknowingly walked right into them. I was talking with a friend and neighbor one night about my fears of being pregnant with Bree. She mentioned she still had one of those at-home heart rate monitors from when she was pregnant. I'd thought about getting one of those when I was pregnant with Chase, but it was classified in all of those "expecting a baby" books as a nice-to-have—because everything was going to be just fine, remember? I thought about it for a minute and then decided to take her up on her offer to loan me her monitor. It would be a really neat way to hear my baby's heartbeat without having to wait for the next scheduled sonogram, or whenever my insurance deemed it necessary. I mean, it's never enough, am I right?

She brought over the monitor and I tucked it away in my nightstand. When we had talked about it, it sounded like a helpful tool to have. But when I was actually holding it, it was a little bit scary. Initially it seemed like a great way to connect with my growing baby. Now, it seemed more like I was checking to make sure my baby was okay. I was back to wondering if I wanted to use it. I was hanging onto what little blissful ignorance I had left.

But one night, the fears were loud. Marcus and I were lounging on the couch and I started to worry about the last time I'd felt Bree move that night. We decided it could be a good idea to use the monitor to ease the fears a little bit.

We went into the bedroom. I slowly rolled over onto the bed

and Marcus opened the drawer to grab the monitor. There was a sense of urgency in the moment so I don't recall thoroughly reading instructions. The bottom line is we were fragile humans with lots of anxiety and a lack of skill, armed with a gently used medical device. This was a horrible idea.

We moved the wand around for about ten seconds trying to get the feel for it. Ten seconds quickly turned into a few minutes...of silence. We couldn't find the heartbeat. I'm sure there's a disclaimer somewhere on the box that cautions the user that this monitor has been known to cause uncontrollable sobbing. Or at least it should. I was a mess. A recurring theme. I had been giving myself pep talks throughout the pregnancy, telling myself that if something went wrong, I'd be okay. I'd been through it before, so I could do it again. Not exactly uplifting, but I was going more for a slap in the face, "you got this" vibe.

But in that moment, I realized all the feelings I wasn't allowing myself to feel. The feelings that had been stuffed deep down because if I didn't acknowledge them, maybe it would hurt less if this didn't work out. In those uncontrollable sobs, I realized just how badly I wanted to keep my baby. I didn't want to feel like I had to have my head in the game. I was tired.

I was tired of grief. I was tired of being sad. I was tired of feeling disconnected from people. I was tired of trying to show everyone I was okay.

I was also terrified. I was terrified that in a matter of minutes I could go from "I got this" to "I can't go through this again—it will break me." I was terrified that maybe God interpreted my feelings of being disconnected as being ungrateful and losing another child was my punishment.

As much as I thought I was detached from this pregnancy, I really wasn't. In that moment it went from being a pregnancy to being *my baby*. My daughter. *I was already madly in love with my daughter and at that moment I thought she was gone.*

Through the fog of my tears, I saw these same fears in Marcus's eyes. While I was on the verge of hyperventilating and sucking snot back into my nose, his steady hand kept trying.

And finally, on the very side of my body, toward the start of my back, we heard it. The heartbeat. She was still here.

We never used that machine again. I thought about taking it out to the driveway and running it over with my car 2,675 times, but it was a loaner. I gave it back to my friend instead. Not nearly as satisfying, but it was nice to have my emotions (kinda) under control again.

Even with so many emotions already at the surface, I still wanted to be "more" during my pregnancies after Chase.

More joyful. More grateful. More relaxed.

More upbeat. More engaged.

Sure, I felt these emotions at different times, but definitely not for prolonged periods. It was really about the pressure to show more of them—for other people. I wanted to reassure people that I was okay. Sometimes it was because I didn't want people to worry. Sometimes it was because seeming like I had it all under control helped avoid awkward and unpredictable conversations. I avoided eye contact with other pregnant women. I didn't feel a camaraderie with fellow baby bumpers. I was an outcast hiding a secret no one wanted to hear. Not that they knew that.

I imagine my outsider status is what a superhero feels like—not being able to share who they really are. Except instead of hands that shoot spider webs like Spiderman, my superpower was...child loss? Hands that shoot spider webs are way cooler—and probably easier to explain. You're right, this is a bad example. I didn't feel like I fit in with new moms and I also didn't fit in with moms who were pregnant with their second, third, etc. I wasn't going to be juggling the demands of a newborn and a young toddler. I was juggling doubts and unstable emotions. The last thing I'd want to do is ruin another mom's ignorant bliss. It hadn't been that long ago that I had that same bliss. I missed that feeling and it deserves all the joy. But I felt the pressure to show more.

Have you ever been driving on the freeway and a car changes lanes in front of you with little warning and no blinker? It's nothing super dangerous, but it ranks pretty high on the rudeness meter. It usually warrants a sarcastic remark like "Oh, hi! Sure, come on over" or "Wonderful, thanks for the blinker." Grief is kinda like rude drivers. Grief is not always reckless; sometimes it's more unassuming and inconveniently swerves into your lane and cuts you off.

Sometimes I'd start the day feeling like I wanted to give more and then I'd get unexpectedly cut off. I'd hear a baby cry at the table next to me at a restaurant, or I'd run into the lady at the grocery store who asks a lot of questions.

It is not lost on me that being pregnant after loss is an amazing gift. But it is not without its own complicated set of emotions. Grief becomes intertwined into everything after loss. It can be a heart-healthy healing process, but it can also be the unavoidable a-hole driver that swerves into your lane on a good day.

When you get cut off, don't get off the road. I give you permission to pull over for a bit to compose yourself, but then just ease back into the slow lane. You don't have to be "more" for anyone.

SEVEN - FA LA LA LA LET'S JUST SKIP IT

I'VE HEARD IT REFERENCED as the year of firsts. There are so many hurdles to get over during that first year after a loved one dies. In my year of firsts, it felt like I was starting over in a lot of ways. Things I was used to doing now seemed scary and new. Holidays were especially challenging. The ones that I once thought were my favorites were unrecognizable. The ones that were never really my favorite became even less enjoyable.

I've never liked Halloween. The smell of mass market milk chocolate combined with the odor of plastic masks is pretty nauseating. It's a day where everyone is hiding behind a costume and pretending to be something they're not. I'm someone who desires to share way too much of herself with the world (like writing this book), so Halloween is literally the opposite of that. I'm never in a hurry to answer the doorbell for trick-or-treaters. It doesn't matter how cute they are. I have concerns with people entering my personal space. Marcus is always tasked with answering the door while I take peeks from the couch, in between sips of wine. You'll hear an occasional "aww" slip out from my mouth, but as soon as the door shuts I wonder if 6:00 p.m. is considered too early to shut off the porch light. I love how approachable I'm sounding right now.

The year Chase passed away, neither one of us were looking forward to answering that door. I didn't have any "awws" in me and the thought of having small child after small child show up at our doorstep sounded, well, torturous.

113

As I started to feel bad for not being in the spirit, I remembered something that our grief counselor shared with us. It's okay to be selfish in grief. This is so incredibly profound that I feel like I have to say it again for the people in the back. *It's okay to be selfish in grief.* Write it down if you need to. Get a Mike Tyson face tattoo about it. Just get behind it. I use this mantra as a hall pass even a decade later.

There is an overly abundant pressure to be "okay" when someone you love dies. We're all supposed to be "fine." If this is the expectation, then actually taking time, let alone *more* time for yourself, seems self-indulgent. Almost...unnecessary? Well, I'm going on record that your "more time" is absolutely necessary. Don't let societal pressure move you into being fine—at least not too early. Take time to do things you feel like doing. No judgment. The only requirement is that it makes your day a little more manageable. The tough moments might become a little less heavy and your heart might feel a little bit more protected. Grief is deeply personal and so you need time to figure out how you are feeling about it. Not how you're feeling compared to someone else. Not how you think others expect you to feel. If you find yourself spending your time doing things others want you to do, that might be a good time to take a pause. Don't forget to ask yourself what you want to do. Take that cruise to escape for a bit. Attend the comedy show even if you think others will question your sanity. Hide in your closet and ugly cry for a few hours. RSVP "no" to the wedding because you're just not loving love at the moment. Write off the upcoming holidays. Whatever you choose to do or not do, *it's not wrong.* It's perfectly alright.

If we didn't have it in us to participate in Halloween, then why do it? But where could we go to escape the peppering sound of our doorbell?

The Olive Garden seemed like a good option. I mean, nothing soothes the soul like a basket of endless breadsticks, am I right?

I know this may come as a shock, but Marcus and I started our spooky Thursday night dinner date at the Olive Garden bar while we waited for our table. We ended up running into one of my coworkers. It was less than ideal, but way better than the Halloween stress we were working on releasing. We exchanged a few niceties and as he headed back to his table I commenced judging people from atop our little bistro table. Between Marcus and me, I'm more of the people watcher.

It might be because I was never really a fan of Halloween, but I really enjoyed purposefully ignoring the holiday. I felt such a sense of relief. I didn't have to pretend—at least not on a grand scale. I mean, I still lied and said I was doing good when the waiter introduced himself and asked, "How are you doing tonight? Can I start you off with some drinks?" It was a resounding "yes" on the drinks, by the way.

Anywhere Else But Here, Please

We weren't the first people to ignore a holiday after loss. Our grief counselor told us she went on a cruise the first Christmas after her son died. I pictured myself on that cruise ship several times. Middle of the ocean, no cell phone reception. It sounded glorious, but we didn't take the cruise.

When Marcus and I talked about how we wanted to spend the holiday season that first year, I envisioned purchasing a ticket aboard the beautiful new cruise liner named *Anywhere Else But Here* and Marcus wanted to keep all of our family plans. Not an ideal time to be on different pages, but we'd work through it. I was already spending these times without Chase, so I definitely wasn't going to voluntarily spend them without Marcus. When Marcus talked about being with our family for the holidays it was with such conviction. Like he needed it. I was still trying to play the role of escape artist. If it was going to inflict hurt, cause me to feel like I was on display, or set me up to potentially cry in front of an audience, I was okay with going into hiding. I didn't care an awful lot about if people thought this was the unhealthiest option. After all, they wouldn't be there. I knew, deep down, that I probably needed family, too. But I was getting really comfortable in my loneliness. So we kept our family plans: a holiday fundraising event, seeing my family for Thanksgiving, and being with his family for Christmas.

Every year, on the weekend before Thanksgiving, we stay with my in-laws. My mother-in-law is part of an organization that hosts an annual pre-Christmas fundraiser that benefits women and girls. There's a Christmas tree raffle and a catered lunch held at the local fairgrounds. It's a big production for a great cause. While I'm at the fundraiser, Marcus golfs with his brother and their friends. We stuck with this tradition.

It was the morning of the fundraiser. My mother-in-law had left her house early to start setting up for the event and Marcus had ducked out for his full day of golfing. I had the house to myself. The thought of having a little time to myself to breathe sounded nice. Little did I know, that time to myself would end up being the thing that made breathing seem so impossible. Hello, Irony. It wouldn't be the last time that giving myself "room to breathe" was a slippery slope into a downward spiral of hyperventilation and tears. It's like in baseball, when an outfielder tries to catch a fly ball on an extremely sunny day. They swirl around the field, confidently repeating, "I got it, I got it, I got it" until it sharply turns to defeat and a "Nope, I don't got it."

As I was putting on my makeup I was thinking about how the day was going to go. Hundreds of women in one place, ringing in the start of the Christmas season. All of them would be chatting with friends and hoping for a chance to win a special tree. I gotta be honest. I didn't want to chat, and I definitely didn't want a tree.

It's a little chaotic when you first enter the fairgrounds arena. You have to buy your tickets, make your way through the crowds, locate your table number, find your empty seat, and then get in line to look at all the trees just out of reach. I usually run into several people I know. One of our family friends had just had a baby and she would be bringing her. Our babies should have been there together. I had planned on it.

I wondered how the people I knew would look at me. Would I be able to see their sad eyes? Would they acknowledge that this was really tough for me? Would everyone just keep their interactions at surface level? Why exactly was I putting myself through this?

As I continued getting ready in my in-laws' guest bathroom, the questions in my head were mounting and so was my temperature. I could feel the warmth welling up inside my body and the tight knot in the pit of my stomach that was slowly working its way up my chest and into my throat. My feet felt heavier than cinder blocks. My chin started to quiver and my eyes were filling up with salt water. I knew if the tears ran over the rims of my lower eyelids, I'd have to start over with the makeup. I'm pretty low maintenance, so that would be the easy fix. But there were bigger risks at play. What if the tears kept coming? What if I lost all stability?

"Don't blink, Laura. *Do not blink.* Don't you do it."

If I couldn't get through a morning with just myself, how the heck was I going to get through the day? I couldn't do this.

Crap, I blinked.

The rush of emotions as they went up my throat and spread over my face and through my limbs was intense. I imagine I looked a little like Dustin Hoffman in *Rain Man*, pacing around the upstairs hallway between the bathroom and the guest room. "I can't do this. Yeah, I definitely can't do this."

I just wanted to be done. I wanted to crawl into the bed, I wanted to shut the door and I wanted to just hide out until this grief business was over. I didn't want to see the sad eyes. I didn't want to slap on a smile. I didn't want to be in these stupid clothes. I didn't, I didn't, I didn't. Probably a good thing we *didn't* buy those holiday cruise tickets. That would have been quite the investment just to curl up like a sad armadillo in a bed below deck.

I picked up my cell phone and called Marcus. Part of me was looking for permission to get back into bed and part of me just wanted him to give me a pep talk. The kind of pep talk where the coach taps the players butt with a "go get 'em!" as they head back onto the field. He was too far away for that butt tap, but he reminded me to breathe and told me that he loved me. He's given better pep talks, but I took it. I knew his golf game wasn't going to be easy either.

Shortly after we got off the phone, my sister-in-law arrived at the house so we could carpool to the event. I got her up to speed as much as I could about my hesitations and worries, but the bulk of my intense freak-out was behind me. I did mention it was a good thing (for her) that she didn't arrive five minutes earlier. At least she knew what cards I was holding going into this thing. She'd been warned. Hey, sometimes you just need to get it out in order to keep going.

My Presence Was the Victory That Day

There was a picture taken at the event that day. I'm sitting at our luncheon table with my sisters-in-law and Marcus's cousins. As I scroll the faces in retrospect it's honestly hard to look at myself for too long. I can see the aftermath of that morning's tears and panic. I lovingly see a girl holding onto some baby weight without her baby. I see a girl in a lot of pain. I don't think reapplying any amount of makeup would have covered all of that. I'd like to say that I was proud of myself for going to the event, but the most profound thing I can say is that I was there. I somehow got from that bathroom to that table and into my seat. I went through the motions. Don't get me wrong, this definitely counts as a trophy moment. It was really freakin' hard and exhausting. But when I look at that picture it's like I see myself, but I wasn't there. It's not me. It's someone who was lost and hurting and who was there physically but not emotionally. And that's more than fine. It was the first holiday event and it was a start. A fine start. It's okay that the most positive thing I can say about it is that it's done.

And yes, I feel like I did get some sad and awkward eyes from people who know me, but I also realized just how much people like raffles and Christmas trees. Going someplace with lots of sparkle and distraction has its advantages. I didn't have to linger in each moment for too long before someone got distracted. "Oh my gosh, is that an iPad under that tree?!"

My in-laws gifted the family with Christmas ornaments dedicated for Chase later that day, before going to dinner. It was a beautiful silver star ornament, etched with Chase's name, and strung up by a silky red ribbon. The emotion of it all sent me heading to the bedroom. You know I don't like feeling like I'm being stared at. What I hadn't thought through was that I'd eventually have to come out of the bedroom to go to dinner. The notion of reentry had me feeling like I was going to be stepping out onto the main stage. It kind of defeated the purpose of trying to hide out in the first place. Marcus had come to the bedroom to check on me. We held hands and walked out of the bedroom together. I've always been a fan of the buddy system.

I kept my head down in my best effort to try to pretend I hadn't just had a total meltdown (again). I know it was "just with family," but it was different. Unlike with my own brother, Marcus's brothers hadn't seen me struggle to learn to ride my bike, or make really bad decisions in high school, or cry when I'd had my heart broken on too many occasions to count. I felt like this was the first time they were really seeing me and I was feeling a bit—okay, very—uncomfortable about it.

As we made our way outside to go to dinner, I kept my head down and consequently lost sight of Marcus. As I lifted my head to cross the street, I could see my brothers-in-law walking toward me. I had a few seconds to process what I thought would happen next. Maybe they'd tease me for completely losing it. Not meanly or anything, but to break up the tension (mine, not theirs). Instead, without hesitation, they hugged me. Fun fact—hugs are a nice way to break up tension, too. At that moment, I didn't have to worry about getting closer to them. We were literally as close as we could be. I'm sure we had hugged at my wedding or something, but these were the hugs I'll never forget. The kind of hug that lingers where, even after the person steps away, you still feel something of theirs stayed with you—comfort, some mutual understanding, an offering, or something I perhaps didn't realize I needed but they could give. These are the hugs we all deserve.

We all made it to the restaurant. We arrived at our table and there was a little bit of chaos as we all tried to figure out who was sitting next to whom. As we dispersed the menus, a wave of silence came over the table as we all started to stare intently at what to order. In true holiday fashion, it had been at least a good two hours since we last ate and we were hungry. I was looking down at my menu, with my head resting in my arms. I heard a couple of requests at the other end of the table for children's menus for my nieces and nephews. I immediately thought that I should be requesting the kids' menu too. I should have been sitting at the outside edge of the table so that I could be near the high chair. Instead, I was a few seats into the row, only needing to worry about my own meal. Still looking down, I let a few tears sneak out before composing myself. It was too late though; my mother-in-law and sister-in-law saw me. And then I saw their tears, too. We smiled, wiped our eyes, and placed our orders. It was an act of solidarity. You stop crying. No, *you* stop crying.

You Can't Go around Grief

That pre-Thanksgiving weekend hadn't been an easy introduction to the holidays. It housed moments I inevitably had to suffer through. I don't mean suffer as if I was treated poorly or subjected to things I could have avoided. I mean suffer as in grief makes you trudge right through the really hard stuff because as much as you may be a master of avoidance, you're not allowed to go around it. There's no shortcut. A panic attack (or twelve) was inevitable. It just happened to be in my in-laws' guest bathroom. Figuring out how to navigate gatherings with extended family and friends, there was no "if" on that one, but "when." If we had canceled our plans, they wouldn't have been avoided, but delayed. As I said earlier, delaying is a totally valid option because you're allowed to be selfish. But I would have missed some of those sweeter moments—like the good hugs.

With that first trip under my belt, it was time for Thanksgiving.

We spent Thanksgiving in San Diego that year visiting my brother's family. It was Marcus, my parents, my brother, my sister-in-law, and my nieces. Thanksgiving was usually local for us, but Marcus and I liked the idea of changing the setting. Again, it wasn't a cruise, but a five-hour drive in southern California traffic could be deemed a voyage. Prior to sitting down for our big meal, I had received several text messages from old friends. The long text chain from college girlfriends of "Happy Thanksgiving" broke when it reached me. I looked down at the messages, but I didn't respond. Cheryl sent a longer text asking for more information about how I was doing. I mean, she knew in general how I was doing, but she was checking in on my mental state at that moment. As my best friend, her "How are you doing?" was not the same as someone else's. Yet, I still didn't respond. I'd already tried the whole panic thing, so I was now going for total shutdown mode. What if I did share my honesty? Is that what people really wanted to hear?

"Happy Thanksgiving! By the way, fun fact, I'm neither happy nor thankful. Gobble gobble!"

So I decided it was best to stay to myself. As we all shuffled around the kitchen, putting the last items on the table before sitting down to eat, I could feel the holiday nervousness kick in. I started to feel that ball in my throat, like I did in my in-laws' bathroom a week earlier, as I started thinking about sitting around the table and having to share what I'm thankful for. I could feel the tears coming—again.

I wasn't busy preparing a little plate for Chase. I only had to worry about myself—again. And let's not forget about the guilt and shame I was feeling for not wanting to shout from the rooftops that I was thankful to be pregnant with my little girl. I was *so extremely thankful* for her; but as you may recall, before our sucky at-home ultrasound incident, I was already preparing myself for something to go wrong. My sadness was just too over-powering and it was smothering any piece of positive emotion that tried to get in on the action. Carrying all the feelings and trying to tend to them all was an impossible task, so I didn't try. I picked the biggest emotion and stuck with that. All I could think was that this wasn't how things were supposed to be.

We kept the talk of thankfulness and blessings short that year. No one was put on the spot and we didn't go around the table one by one. It was more of a group speech. We were spit-balling ideas that all had a common theme. We were all holding back tears while we announced that we were all thankful for each other. I was self-absorbed in my own grief, but I did have moments of wondering what grief was still feeling like for oth-ers. My parents had lost their grandson. My brother and sister-in-law lost their nephew and my nieces only have a few pictures with their cousin.

Propellers Can't Touch Each Other—or Can They?

Cheryl had designated herself as my very own Turkey Day stalker—one thing I was extremely thankful for. When she didn't get responses to the numerous text messages she'd sent me, she went a different route. She called my mom. Yup, while others were giving me space (grief's more natural response), she was all up in my business.

Do you remember P.E. class in elementary school? The teacher would have the class spread out on the blacktop. Then we'd be instructed to reach our little chicken arms out to the sides and twist our bodies from left to right. If our fingers, now the tips of our propellers, touched the person/helicopter next to us, we were too close together and we'd have to adjust accordingly. That distancing method is how I was approaching friendships. I wanted to see you on the blacktop but I wanted to be far enough away that we couldn't touch. It's been a decade and I still do this. I also realize that it's hard to recover from pushing people away for a really long time. Losing friendships is the risk I unknowingly took because I couldn't do anything else.

Cheryl wasn't having any part of this philosophy. If we're sticking with the P.E. class analogy, she had managed to sneak through the space below my outstretched chicken arms and wedged herself lovingly underneath my armpit. If she hadn't done that when she did, I believe I would have successfully moved her to the other side of the blacktop where I'd pushed everyone else. My mom picked up her phone call. I could hear the exchange of niceties and then my mom told Cheryl, "Yeah, she's right here." I could hear her stumbling through some other words after that. Most likely Mom was trying to be cryptic about how well I was (not) doing without giving me something to sink my snippy daughter teeth into. We assured Cheryl that I was as good as could be expected but not to worry; I hadn't gone off any sort of proverbial deep end and no search party was needed.

Time can naturally change our friendships. So maybe my avoidance was merely speeding up the inevitable morphing of relationships as we all grow up and put more physical space between us. Maybe it wasn't. It's kind of hard to say. The definition of my family had forever changed, so it's not really surprising that I would feel changed in other aspects of my life. Different and distant.

This wasn't just another example of a holiday gone through. This was the beginning of new holidays. The way it would be. The holidays of *always missing Chase*.

The Four-Way Stop Dance

On Christmas morning, I leaned over the second-floor railing and saw a choo-choo train set up for my nephew. There wasn't an easy way for this day to happen. Marcus and I didn't want people to cancel Christmas. Okay, maybe that's not entirely true, but it's not completely false either. I don't think Chase would have wanted that either. I just think he would have really loved that train set and I would have loved to watch him discover it on Christmas morning.

Marcus and I stayed upstairs as long as possible, anxiously shuffling from the guest room to the bathroom to get ready before his sister and brothers and their families arrived. I don't think I've ever taken so long to get myself "holiday ready." If there were a way to brush each hair on my head individually and be held up with that trivial task for the next 24 hours, I would have done it. "I'll be down in a minute; I only have 2,368 hairs left!" Marcus and I eventually went downstairs together. We knew we just needed to get through it.

It's not that our family was ignoring the pain of the holiday. We were all very aware of the "suckiness." We were all just trying to figure out how to move through it for ourselves and each other. You know I love my analogies. It's like when you pull up to a four-way stop with three other cars at the same time. You're all looking at each other to figure out who's going to move first. Sometimes everyone's too polite and nobody moves, so you're all just waiting. Eventually someone decides they'll go and they start to roll into the intersection. Only you all had that same idea. So now everyone puts on the brakes again. Then the aggressively polite dance starts. The hands start waving to each other. You go. No, you go! Will someone just go?! By this time it's only three cars at the stop, because one driver has gotten so sick of it all they gunned it and took their chances. Emotionally charged family gatherings can be like four-way stops.

As Marcus and I made our way down to the first floor, the first thing my mother-in-law did was apologize. I think the apology was for the train set we had already seen and for the hurt that the rest of this day was going to bring. I'm not going to lie and say the train set didn't make me mad. I knew that my nephew deserved Christmas. But I also knew that Chase deserved it, too. I wasn't solely mad at that train set. I was actually mad at the train set that wasn't there. A small part of me wondered if I could I still make it in time to board that cruise ship if I left at that moment. I bet they don't have train sets on cruise ships.

Marcus and I got to open presents for Bree that year. She was due in four months. I was still sticking to my guns of no baby shower, so this kinda felt like that shower (although everyone knew not to call it that). We opened boxes of cute outfits and comfy blankies. I had been so nervous to celebrate our little girl. I was actually surprised at how nice it felt to embrace the happiness that having a baby can bring. I enjoyed seeing the family smile and it felt good to give myself permission to do the same. I hadn't realized how much I'd been fighting with my emotions the previous six months. I was tired. The smile came easier when I knew it was something my daughter deserved. The moment wasn't over the top. It was kind. It was polite. It was safe. It was nice.

I want to make sure I'm not confusing things here. Yes, the smile and the time with family was a really nice moment for me. But that doesn't mean I'm admitting in any way that all the tears, the freak-outs, the comfort I had with sitting in complete and utter sadness was somehow too much. The pain was never silly or poured on too thick. The only times I may have let a doubt like that creep in was because I was worried about what other people would think. *But other people didn't lose their child.* It was all necessary—all of it. I've never looked back at this time and thought, "Geez, Laura, you should have just been happier." I couldn't be happier—for myself or anyone else. When you're going through it, the emotions just come. There are times when you can control them and times when you can't. Or when you won't. Because to try and be something for someone else—or to try and fool yourself—is not going to work.

For a really long time I let sadness lead because, very simply put, that's what showed up. I needed to let it lead. To push it away or sack it up wasn't going to help anyone. Most importantly, it wasn't going to help me. People who have had a loved one die ask me for advice. I have a really hard time telling others that it will get better or easier or whatever awkwardly generic word you want to use. I wholeheartedly believe that it will, but saying that would diminish the storm of all the emotions that will hit before things start to feel a little bit better. The waves will crash into you and you'll wonder when you'll ever be able to catch your breath again—that is the time reserved *only* for the grieving. My suggestion is don't use that time to figure out how you should feel or trying to get on with life. Your grieving time is a time reserved for whatever you truly feel. So, yes, opening those gifts was a nice moment. But it was that way because it happened at the right time and when I was ready to feel it.

January and Sprinkles

On the heels of all these year-end holidays, Chase's birthday is January 5th. In the weeks and days leading up to his birthday I tried to figure out what my heart wanted to do to celebrate him.

All I kept thinking was: celebrating him is salt in my wound. But I would come back to reminding myself that I'm his mom and it's my job to make his birthday special. So, cake it is!

I went to the grocery store and picked out the Funfetti Cake mix. There was no question what the cake flavor would be. I grew up on this Pillsbury classic. What's better than sprinkles on a cake? Yup, sprinkles *in* a cake. Bravo, Pillsbury, bravo (*insert slow clap followed by a dramatic rise to a standing ovation*).

I'm not a baker, but I can follow directions on a box. Okay, fine, as long as it's five ingredients or less. You got me—make it four or less. Standing in my kitchen, I measured, poured, dumped, cracked, and got ready to mix. As I started to swirl it all together, my mood changed. As I watched it all coming together in batter form, the voices inside my head entered the room. It wasn't a big kitchen, so I didn't necessarily welcome the extra visitors. Yet again, grief just shows up. I started to wonder who was going to eat all this cake. Should I get a birthday candle? Who would blow it out? Should I sing Happy Birthday? I had a different theme song playing in my head ("It's Your Party and I'll Cry if I Want To"). I never thought I'd be making a sad birthday cake. Until now, I didn't even know that was a thing. As the batter started coming together it felt thick, and the speed of my spoon was slowing to a sluggish churn. I knew if I stopped stirring I'd have less distraction and it would just be me and my thoughts. I decided to let them unfold as they may (or maybe in baking terms this is actually "folding"?). After all, it was just me, grief, and sprinkles. I cried over the mixing bowl and purposefully let a few tears fall into it. Maybe that was my secret ingredient. My own physical interpretation of "made with love."

I had seen so many ideas posted on the internet about how to celebrate your angel baby's birthday. I wanted to be able to handle this. I loved the idea of the birthday cake and I did believe with all of my heart that Chase should get his cake. I finished making the cake. In my mind, I had envisioned Marcus and I each taking half of that 9"x13" cake and eating every crumb. But we didn't. We each had a piece of a square. One bite each. That's all we could get down. And no, it wasn't because it was dry, *thankyouverymuch*.

These days, we always have dessert for Chase's birthday. I just don't make it. Parenting tip: nothing is better because you made things harder on yourself than they needed to be. Even if it's not homemade, your child will still love it—and you.

I'm able to safely look back on those first holidays without Chase and see that even though I was a mess—angry, sad, confused, and tired—it was all part of the process of discovering a different feeling of joy for my future. It's been a process of letting go of what I thought was going to be my joy and making room to embrace all the joys that would unfold in the years to come. I just had to find some space for them. There has been joy in finding my resilience. The joy of being proud of how far I've come. The joy of finding so much love in the present and still honoring the pieces of my pain. I can say "Merry Christmas" now, even though a piece of my "Merry" will always be missing. I can say "Happy Thanksgiving" now, without all the pieces of me being completely thankful for some pieces of my story. The big picture is still a huge gift and the present can still be filled with beauty. The pain is not going away, so I continue to build up around it. With each holiday, new memory, and next life milestone, I'm building up my fortress of new love and joy. It's almost protecting the pain so that we can all coexist.

Building anything is not without struggle. Those first years and holidays, it's safe to say I felt like a home that had been knocked down to the studs. I felt raw, exposed, beat-up, and without direction. Have you ever stood in an unfinished house and wondered if you were standing in the future bathroom or the master bedroom? I have a horrible sense of direction, and grief can leave me wondering where the heck I am and where I should go. But it doesn't matter. I'm the Builder. I can knock it down, build it back up, change the layout, cry, laugh, acknowledge, ignore, and still throw in some dang sprinkles (but only if it feels right, of course).

EIGHT - PORTA POTTIES BUILD FRIENDSHIPS

WHEN I WAS PREGNANT with Chase I looked forward to having other mom friends. I pictured us getting together on the weekends with the kids. We could talk about our woes, give each other advice, laugh, and find comfort that the things we'd been worried about for the past week are "perfectly normal."

When Chase was born, I got to experience what I'd hoped for. There were stroller walks with friends and their kids and lunchtime play dates to watch our babies wiggle on the floor while us moms talked about the challenges of breastfeeding.

After Chase died, I didn't have mom friends anymore. Sure, I still had these friends who were moms, but all of them still had their babies. I didn't feel like I could lean on them because I wasn't like them anymore. I always wondered: if I was having a rough day of grieving and called one of them to talk, would I be placed on hold while they were trying to tackle nap time? Would they have to put the phone down while they heated up another bottle? I wasn't part of that group anymore. I was an awkward interruption. Just imagining the possibility of hearing the sound of a friend's baby on the other end of the line could put me into tears. Why would I put myself in a position for the possibility of more pain? So instead I avoided phone calls or check-ins with friends when it all felt like it was too much to handle. I was carrying my pain and I was also protecting it so it didn't get bigger. If I wanted support, I decided I'd have to look somewhere else. I'd just learned how to use those elementary school propeller arms again, so I might as well keep them in rotation (pun intended).

The Search

After preliminary autopsy results mentioned the congenital heart defects, I started doing some research on ways to get involved with this cause. I came across a national organization that focuses on raising funds for research in support of children born with heart defects. I initially felt like I'd hit the motherlode. Maybe this is where I'd find my new mom friends. A local chapter was hosting an introductory phone call to talk about their fundraising efforts and meet potential new members. I was a little hesitant to join the call, being that at the time it had only been a matter of weeks since Chase passed away. But if this was my chance to meet other moms who had lost their children too, then I needed to try.

The afternoon of the call, I rushed home from the grocery store, dropping bags on the kitchen floor as I was scrambling to dial in. The call started. In addition to feeling flustered and sweaty from trying to fit in my quick trip to the store, I was feeling very hopeful, knowing that I would be "surrounded" by these moms. My optimism grew as I listened about the great work the organization was doing. These could be my people. At the end of the call the moderator welcomed callers to introduce themselves. I didn't want to be the first one to chime in. I decided I'd let a few women speak and then I'd politely take my turn.

One by one the moms spoke up. They gave their name and then their "why" for being on the call that day.

"My name is _____ and my heart warrior is _____."

For context, there are warriors (children living with and fighting their conditions) and there are angels (children who have died).

I am not trying to diminish the fight of any warrior, but after every warrior was mentioned, I kept wondering where my angels were. My initial strategy of chiming in after a few women spoke changed to just waiting it out until after the first mom shared about the loss of her child. Except that introduction never came. So, inevitably, I would be last to speak. All of these moms had children who were alive? The anxiety about sharing had steadily been increasing with every new voice. I didn't have much practice yet telling people that my son had just died. I was quickly going back and forth between "I'm going to confidently blurt it out to show them how proud I am to be Chase's mom" to "if I hang up now no one will ever know that I was the rude caller who bounced."

"Anyone else we didn't get to?" the moderator chimed in.

Silence. Then I went.

"Umm, hi, my name is Laura. I'm on the call today because my son Chase died a few weeks ago and...." Aaaaand I blacked out. Okay, I didn't really black out, but what came next was a blubbering mess.

All of these moms had been fighting for and with their children for years. All I kept thinking was that I didn't even get a chance to fight for my son. I got a phone call while sitting at my desk at work and an autopsy that gave me anything but closure. My cause going forward seemed like it was a small dot on a blurry dart board.

The moms on the call that day were warm, fierce, and carrying their own heaviness. They were moms I looked up to, but they weren't my moms.

What does that say about me that I couldn't find it in my

heart to give back to a good cause? That I didn't want to use Chase's life as a platform to save other children? I hung up feeling like complete poop. And speaking of poop...remember the porta potty we'd parked on our front lawn for Chase's memorial "after-party"? It was actually the ticket to finding my mom group.

A Friendly Interrogation

After I'd posted to my neighborhood Facebook page on the day of Chase's funeral to warn of the added traffic near our house, I expected a few responses to offer condolences. What I hadn't expected was a private message, sent to my inbox, that would save my life.

Jamie lived down the street and her daughter, Naya, had died two years earlier. I remember receiving Jamie's message and getting so excited to tell my husband. She told me about Naya and that she was available if I ever wanted to talk. It was like finally finding Waldo on the page of Where's Waldo, after staring at a sea of almost familiar faces. Or finding that last puzzle piece you were sure got left out of the box at packaging, only to discover that it had fallen and was hiding under the table leg. For the record, Jamie is way hotter than Waldo.

I got to meet Jamie twelve days after Chase passed away. It was after the memorial and after people had all gone back home. She came over to our house after work one day to say hi and share some books she had found helpful during those initial days and months of grief. Before she arrived I felt like I was waiting for a blind date. It wasn't until I knew that she was actually on her way over that I realized just how much hope I had in this connection.

I was excited, nervous, pacing, and trying to keep my cool. She knocked on our front door and as I opened it up the emotions took hold and I took hold of her—literally. I didn't just give her a hug. I was hanging on. I was swimming in uncharted waters and I'd just found a buoy. A very petite buoy. She probably wondered if I was ever going to let go. I honestly didn't know if I wanted to. Maybe I'd just end up swallowing her. I eventually did—let go, that is.

She came into the house and talked with Marcus and me for a little while. My parents were still in town after the funeral and sitting at the kitchen table. The quiet observers. They were probably thinking their daughter should be playing more hard to get. Totally kidding, I'm sure they were just as relieved as I was and, truth be told, playing hard to get was never my strong suit. Jamie let Marcus and me ask questions and she listened. It brings me to tears just thinking about it. It was an amazingly indescribable feeling to discover I wasn't alone. Plainly put, it was lifesaving.

So how was *she* feeling in those moments? Oh, for her, it probably felt more like a panel interview. Heck, probably an interrogation. I wanted to know if everything I was feeling was normal. What was okay? What wasn't? What should I prepare myself for? I wanted so badly for it all to be clearly laid out so that I didn't have to expend any more emotional energy to get through this.

It's as if I was really saying "Here. Here's all my sh*t. Can you please just take it, move some things around if you have to, and give it back to me with a plan attached?"

Jamie talked to me about some other child loss moms in the area with whom she'd become friends over the last few years. They would get together from time to time. She invited me to their meetups several times before I finally said yes. It took me a little while to be ready. I don't even know what "ready" really means. From an outsider's perspective, I fit the general criteria:

Child who passed away? Check.

I think the piece of me that wasn't ready was the part of me that didn't want to believe that this was all happening. To be in a room with another mom whose child had passed away was comforting. To be in a room with a gaggle of moms? Well, that's just overwhelming. There was something a little intimidating about going from "I know someone else" to "I'm part of a community." Maybe that's another reason I didn't want to participate in the children's heart organization. It was hard to admit that I was actually part of something bigger that carried so much sadness.

Jamie was a refreshingly open book, but she did have one hesitation. She told me that she had a rainbow baby and that one of the other moms in their group was pregnant. She knew these things might be upsetting to me. I couldn't believe that somebody else could actually understand that seeing a baby or a baby bump could be upsetting to another person. Her understanding was a gift.

As I mentioned in the introduction, Jamie's mention was the first time I learned the term "rainbow baby." The first time I ran into Jamie with her rainbow baby, I was coming home from work. I was pulling my car into the driveway and she was coming around the street corner with her baby stroller. As soon as she saw me, she quickly tried to cover up the stroller and her young son. I'm pretty sure she would have pushed the stroller into the bushes if I'd wanted her too. We laughed as she tried to bring the sunshade of the stroller down as far as it could go—and then farther down than that. It reminded me of *The Wizard of Oz*. Pay no attention to the man behind the curtain! I assured her that it was okay and that the sight of her with her son wasn't making me sad.

And it really was okay.

I had been out on several occasions where even the sound of

a baby crying had me feeling an ache in my tummy and a lump in my throat. But this was different.

Society tells us that we should *ooh* and *aah* over babies. It's not about you, it's about the baby. Smile at the baby or you're rude. Ignore them and you must be a miserable person.

With Jamie, we understood and laughed over the loving avoidance. We weren't miserable people. We were grieving moms. There was no mustering of a smile and no hurt feelings over the absent oohs and aahs. The genuine laughter and mutual appreciation of her "you don't have to do any of that" vibe was the greatest display of a "no, I love *you* more" kinda love.

Maybe I could get behind being a part of *this* community. After months of politely rejected invitations and silent tears, I accepted Jamie's next and approximately eighth invitation to meet the moms' group.

The night Jamie was picking me up, I waited at the front door like I had done when I first met her. I was scared, nervous, and excited. Marcus could tell I was anxious and he kept encouraging me to have a great time. I know that he was happy for me but I was really sad to be leaving him. We'd been getting through this together. Our grief counseling had been together. Our "happy hours" after work were just the two of us. It didn't feel right leaving him, but he understood the desire for healing and connection. I wanted him to have a dads' group. I hoped that I could come home later that night and share something new and beautiful with him.

After Friends

I saw Jamie's car pull up. Okay, here we go.

As I got in the car and we started to drive away, I told Jamie that I had something to share.

"You're pregnant," she said.

"I am. It's really early though." I sounded like I was defending the fact that it could all wash away at any moment. I didn't have to say that, because we both knew that was true.

She was so happy for me and reminded me that one of the moms who was going to be there that night was about twenty-four weeks pregnant. We could talk all about it. I loved that idea. I remember walking through the doorway of Samantha's house and feeling like the ultimate new girl. I didn't know these ladies yet, but they already knew my biggest secret. They not only knew it, they embraced me because of it. I fought the urge to start sobbing immediately, but the feelings of relief that washed over me when I saw their first smiles was life-giving.

I was feeling hopeful, but I wasn't naïve to the fact that these friendships might not work out. Sure, we all had something in common, but that doesn't necessarily seal the deal on a great friendship. I have brown hair. I know lots of people with brown hair, but we're not all besties. Okay, that's probably too general of an example. But what if they grieved differently than I did? I gravitate toward awkward humor. What if they had a "no uncomfortable laughing" policy?

As we sat there at Sam's kitchen table we talked...and we laughed. Genuinely laughed. And cried. It was glorious!

These ladies were my first "after friends." My "after friends" are friendships I've formed after Chase's death. They never got to know me before my greatest grief. They are empathetic, open, and, most importantly, they don't shy away when I talk about Chase. Heck, they actually bring him up. He's not just talked about as my child who died, he's talked about as one of my children. They don't bring him up as an opportunity to insert themselves into my story, but to remind me that they are thinking about him, too, and the ways that he's shaped the friend they see before them. These friends understand that losing him was an event and loving him is an eternity.

I used to talk about Chase with every new relationship opportunity. I'd think to myself, he's my son, so of course I should talk about him whenever I want (for the record, that always remains a true statement). Except a lot of times I would get so sad when the responses I received weren't what I wanted. Sometimes I could tell from the other person's body language that they were uncomfortable with my share. Sometimes they passed on the opportunity to offer condolences. They didn't ask any follow-up questions about what kind of baby Chase was. Whatever it was that rubbed me the wrong way, it would leave me disappointed and honestly unhappy that I'd shared Chase with them at all.

Over the years, I've changed things up a little bit. I hold back on sharing about Chase right outta the gate. I meet someone and I give myself time to feel out the new relationship. Maybe I wait to see if they share something close to their heart. Do they show empathy? Are they a good listener or are they using this conversation as a vessel to hear themselves talk?

Instead of walking into a room naked (metaphorically speaking), I'm wearing my bathrobe with the hope that with just the right audience, I might be able to bare it all (again, a metaphor, but if you're into public nudity, that's cool too).

Over the years, my moms' group has been there every step of the way. We've seen more rainbow babies, more loss, and more grief. There is more to all of our lives than what brought us together, but that's true with all friendships. I'm just so incredibly grateful to know that whenever I walk into a room and they're there, I don't need my metaphorical bathrobe. I can bare it all and just be me. I love you, Jamie, Samantha, Nichole, Dae, and Sarah. I am so grateful for these new friends.

I'm also grateful to have made new connections with old friends.

Rekindling

About two months before Chase passed away, a friend from high school posted on Facebook that her daughter had passed away. I was pregnant with Chase at the time and in the camp of people thinking, "Oh my gosh, I just can't even imagine." Then Chase died. Now, unfortunately, I could imagine.

She was so incredibly thoughtful and messaged me shortly after she saw my Facebook post about Chase's death. She wanted me to know that she was there for me if I ever needed to talk. At the beginning, I didn't. For those first few days, I didn't need to talk about it, because it couldn't possibly be happening. I remember her messages having quite a few exclamation marks. I'm not the punctuation police, but I wondered if this was just an excessive use of exclamation marks or if she *really* wanted me to respond? Without responding, she sent me another message apologizing if she seemed to come off too strong. She didn't need to apologize. I was just emotionally unavailable. I feel like that's how all good romances start. Someone who was once emotionally unavailable comes around and something beautiful starts to happen.

I quickly realized that I needed her as much as she needed me. We became Facebook messaging buddies for the next several years. Through the early months of grief, our pregnancies with our rainbow babies, and the first *angelversaries*. There was no "appropriate" time to reach out. Appropriate, by definition, meant all the time. It was perfectly normal to start "chatting" at 2:00 a.m. about our fears or something someone said that day that made us mad. All of it was up for grabs and we took it. We supported each other and there weren't enough exclamation marks in the world to capture our bond and friendship during that time. Period!

I sometimes wonder if we were meant to meet in high school so we could be there for each other later. I guess that would also mean that Mark Zuckerburg invented Facebook just for us. Maybe he did. I'd like to believe everything started with good intentions.

The intensity of our grief has faded and our lives have become a lot busier over the years, but we have both said that we couldn't have gotten through that time in our lives without each other.

Thank you, Liz, for reaching out when you did...exclamation point!

Reflection

Several years before losing Chase, I had received the news that an old friend and coworker's son had passed away. Danny was in his twenties. When I had heard the news of his passing, I started to write a poem to give to his mom, Audrey. I didn't know what to say but I hoped I could show her that she was in my thoughts in my own way.

I never sent her the poem. I second guessed if it was the right thing to do. I was worried it would make her hurt more. Honestly, I made lots of excuses. Now I know, after the death of my own child, I wasn't trying to protect her, I was trying to protect myself.

I didn't want to feel the grief. She didn't either, but she didn't have a choice.

We were living far apart when Chase passed away, but Audrey enveloped me in many a virtual hug. I didn't feel like I deserved them.

Chase was only six months old and Danny was a young man, but the community of child loss moms does not discriminate. There is no "Well, your son only lived for six months and mine lived for over twenty years." It is a common bond and an insanely supportive community.

I have said before that I can't imagine the pain of losing an older child, with so many memories. And you know what? Those moms of older children have expressed sadness that I was robbed of the opportunity to create so many memories. Ignoring time as an actual unit of measure, the fact is that all of us child loss moms are holding onto and letting go of the possibility of a lifetime of memories.

I'm so grateful that this community doesn't make me feel like my loss is less because of the stand-alone measure of time. There is no comparison game. No one misses their child more than someone else. There is only support and the hope of healing.

I still have that unfinished poem I wrote for Audrey:

An amazing relationship – mother and son
The smiles you have shared never undone
The proud stories that were told of school and beyond
Left us all wanting to have that great bond
A natural mother, comedian and friend
We can't get enough, there is never an end
A strong woman who will get through this tough time
Danny will be watching, a love sublime

I'm not going to lie, at least 99 percent of this makes me cringe. I now know there is no "getting through this." I didn't yet know the bond between a mother and son, let alone child loss. So now, let's try this again (caution, it still rhymes).

For you, Audrey:

I wasn't there when you needed friends to be
I hate that human condition got the best of me
The love that you have with your handsome son
It's preciously all yours but it's infectiously won
The hearts of everyone who feels its great gift
For so many years it has helped me to lift
My head from my hands as I've cried similar tears
I have felt Danny with Chase as a guide through the years
Mom's handsome handyman and life's favorite parts
He's still showing his love through random found hearts
Thank you Audrey for sharing your son
Because the smiles he brings are endless – never ever
undone

A big piece of losing Chase has been about self-reflection. I look back on relationships and circumstances in my life where I could have or should have handled things differently. I can't change the past, but I move forward knowing that I can change my future. I control at least some of my reactions to what comes my way.

Part of grief and loss is experiencing silence in the most unexpected places. One side of the coin is people saying the absolute wrong thing and the other side is people saying nothing at all. When Chase died, I told myself that, going forward, I was going to be the person who potentially says the wrong thing.

Because to me, the silence hurts more. It's a missed opportunity for connection. Or, at its worst, it's confirmation that a friendship wasn't ever that strong to begin with. If the other person doesn't want to pick up what I'm putting down, great. Then at the very least, they have the opportunity to shut me down. Either way, the person who's hurting has the choice.

I'm grateful for the choices people gave me and the connections that came from it. I had my first experiences with this after I wrote the Facebook post sharing that Chase had died.

When Facebook friends read the news of Chase's passing, I heard from many of them. To my surprise, it wasn't all "I'm so sorry for your loss" types of conversations. Sometimes the person shared with me about the loss of their parent or the depression they've been living with (the loss of pieces of themselves). Sure, for a minute I thought, "This is not the same thing." But I'd find myself drawn to these messages. I'd sit on the hard wood bench in my bedroom days after Chase died, typing responses to these friends I hadn't spoken to in years and sometimes decades. As more and more wrote to me about their grief and their hurts, I realized just how much we are all carrying and how much we all need connection.

We all experience grief at some point. By definition, it's a connector. I feel so grateful and honored that these people shared their grief with me. These exchanges happened over a decade ago and I still carry them with me. No, we couldn't bond specifically about child loss, but we had a mutual understanding of the power that grief has.

Grief shapes the person you are and the paths you take, and it can even lead you to rekindling old friendships (the usual social media scroll updates don't count).

Old Friends

I've talked about the unexpected gifts of new and rekindled connections, but it's hardest to talk about the relationships with those who are closest to me. There is a lot of push and pull here that I still struggle with. By default, the people closest to me had the most opportunity to hurt my feelings. But I don't want to sit here and type out the ways I got hurt. The emotions I have around who did what—or didn't do what—took a long time to release. If I had written this book years ago, you could probably have heard me "mad typing" from miles away. Now, in a surprising (at least to me) turn of events, I reflect more on my role in all of the hurt. If you're into labeling it, then one could say that I'm "taking responsibility." It's probably not in the way you'd think. Sure, there are times that I wish I would have handled things differently. But there is still no doubt in my mind that I just couldn't have.

Remember me, I was the girl sitting at the kitchen table playing a game of will-she-eat-the-sandwich? I was relearning how to hold a cup of coffee. I was numb and clouded. I wasn't capable of much and I was incapable of a lot.

I have to constantly remind myself that these are not excuses, but the facts of my grief.

Maybe I should have been more compassionate or understanding about where others were coming from. Maybe I should have kept calling my mom friends even if I felt like I didn't belong anymore. Every time I ask myself these "maybe" questions and think about what it would have entailed to pick up the phone and open myself up to the possibility of hearing a baby on the other end of the line, I get this sinking feeling in my stomach. A nauseating lump in my gut. If I still have this physical reaction even now to the intensity of the pain that I carried back then, how could I have expected myself to act any differently? So, after lots of self-reflection, I've started to cut myself and others some slack.

Yes, friends said the wrong things. Yes, I pushed friends away. Heck, I pushed even when friends did nothing wrong. Any distance I have with friends now, I have to be okay with whatever part I played in getting there. It's not necessarily that I feel regret over how I handled things, it's knowing that I couldn't have done any better at that time so this is where we're at. I wish that Chase hadn't died and opened the door for these darker pieces of grief to work their way in.

Remember that very first Thanksgiving when my best friend Cheryl called and called and called until my mom picked up? She had to do that because I pushed and I pushed *and I pushed.*

I'm sure I was so exhausting. Maybe I still am (no need to weigh in on this one).

I don't know if certain relationships would have stayed strong if Chase hadn't died. Maybe other life forces would have gotten us all to where we're at now anyway. Some relationships lovingly strengthened and others went from extremely close to cordial. I share this not because I'm angry, but because I've learned this is why I'm so protective of my heart in new relationships now. I already have a lot of "I don't knows" and "maybes" when I think about Chase's life and death. If I held onto these "I don't knows" and "maybes" too, my emotional tank would runneth over.

So I put my energy and my love into my now. My now is a place that nurtures new connections, has gratitude for the friendships that strengthened, and has more acceptance for relationships that have gained distance. No, it's not perfect, but my now will always be a place of progress.

Also, I feel it's worth mentioning that the goal of bringing up my moms' group is not to tell you that you have to go out and find new friends. Goodness knows you're already dealing with a lot and I turned their initial offers down anyway. It's more to reassure you that your people are out there. Even if you think they're not. If you're wondering if there's something wrong with you because you think certain things are funny now that the old you could have deemed as sad or uncomfortable, there's absolutely nothing wrong with you. If you're wondering if anyone else has felt the way you're feeling because social media algorithms only show you people who have it all figured out, you're not alone. Not in the slightest. Also, I'm not sure if this is really comforting at this point, but you've always got me.

NINE - FROM BELLY TO BABY

THE THOUGHT CROSSED MY mind a few times that I should stop here. This is where this book should end and a new one should begin. I could have one book about working through the early stages of my grief and one book about what it was like to give birth to my rainbow babies. But that would be the exact opposite of art imitating life. These pieces of my life are so interwoven that separating them on paper wouldn't be fair or accurate. This is my *one* life.

Chase's death has shaped how I look at pregnancy, how I live, who I am, and the relationships I have with my other children. I also think any compartmentalized way of thinking is a product of societal pressure. It's the pressure to acknowledge that this bad thing happened, but now that's over and there's this new happier thing we should focus on. What a wonderfully upbeat and heartbreaking approach that should never be pushed onto anyone. Ever.

Anyone who's experienced profound loss knows that no matter what new things come and no matter how genuinely joyous your outlook is or should be (ahem, society), you'll always carry the grief because the love stays with you forever. It becomes part of your genetic makeup. So it's not love, then loss, then grief, and *then* rainbows. It's love *and* loss *and* grief *AND* rainbows. It's a package deal in this one life.

When I was getting ready to deliver my rainbow babies, there was no question about it—Chase was with me and our whole family. I could feel him with me through every tough conversation, every worry, and every push.

These are the stories of Chase's siblings, Bree and Matthew, coming into my life. They arrived within the two years after Chase died. While I would love to go on and on about each of them, I realize that I may lose you if this book ends up being longer than the Merriam-Webster Dictionary. I would also like to acknowledge and send out a gentle reminder that during this time I was still very fragile and my memories are less linear and more pinball-ish. *Was that the freak-out during Bree's pregnancy or Matthew's delivery?*

It's no contest that these two kiddos are individually magical, but their arrivals share common themes. I'm sticking more with themes here.

New Math

I know I've already touched on this but I feel that it's worth revisiting. Remember my run-in with the nice lady at the grocery store? Have you heard about the "new math" they're teaching in schools today? I agree, I'm not going to learn it either.

Parenting after child loss has its own set of new math rules that are already complicated enough to explain. Yeah, here's some new math for you:

Laura has had four pregnancies. She's had one miscarriage. She's had three live births. One child was born and went to Heaven. Two children are living. How many children does Laura have?

Answer: Laura has however many children Laura decides she's going to say she has.

Some might say it's a trick question. Some might say there is no wrong answer. I'm going to go with the most positive spin (classic people pleaser response) and say every answer is the right one. It might not feel good, but the decision you make isn't ever the issue.

The Bowl of Sticks

I didn't want to have a baby shower when I was pregnant with Bree and Matthew. So I didn't. Was I extremely grateful to be pregnant again? Absolutely! However, a party is an opportunity to celebrate. It's not a requirement. Not having one doesn't make the milestone worthy of celebration any less amazing, and having a party doesn't mean that the milestone is any "more" of anything. Now that I've angered everyone who loves parties, let's keep going.

I wanted to want a party, but forcing it wasn't going to do me much good. In fact, it would probably cause the opposite effect. I know me. I've shared I'm a crier. I hate attention. I'm okay with blending in. I don't want to talk about it (whatever it is) until I do, and I'd sweep the Olympics if overstressing about the tiniest decisions was a professional sport. And this was me even before Chase died. So not having a party was a protective measure. Making that decision made me feel like I had some control during years filled with very little control at all.

So when my coworkers wanted to do something for me before I went out on maternity leave, I allowed them to coordinate a non-baby shower lunch. There were rules. Baby gifts were strictly prohibited and if you said the word "baby," you'd be asked to leave. I'm so fun.

I'm relieved that everyone followed the rules. There were no onesies or soft baby blankets to unwrap. Instead, my coworkers gifted me an orchid. My first thought was that I should enjoy it while it lasts. In a few weeks, the petals will fall off and I'll be left with a bowl of dried up sticks. I'm a horrible plant mom.

I brought my new orchid home, and sure enough one morning I found myself staring at the bowl of sticks. The flowers had fallen off and I was thinking to myself, "Here we go again." But I couldn't help but notice that the dog-eared leaves flopping over the base of the pot were still green. In fact, there was a new, little ear starting to grow. I picked up the sad-looking pot and placed it near the window in my kitchen. Then I did what I do best with all plants. I ignored it. It sat there for months and months and months. I'd water the sticks a tiny bit, when I remembered, and then I'd let it be. One morning, months later, things were a little bit different. A new stick had started to grow. It was green and looked shockingly sturdy for being so petite. Something was happening. For weeks it slowly grew tall and eventually there were new flower buds. These buds eventually opened and I saw flowers again. That's when I had my revelation. I not only like orchids, I *am* an orchid. The orchid is my spirit plant.

For the many long and painful months, my orchid and I were taking some time to repair. We didn't quite know when we'd feel like blooming again, but we did. Our bloom isn't consistent and it isn't forever. Our flowers will fall again, but that just means we need some time. They'll come back when they're ready. I just have to be patient even when all I can see in front of me are sticks.

Yes, I've formed my life's philosophy from an orchid. I highly recommend getting yourself an orchid. Or whatever spirit plant suits your fancy.

Sometimes Gender Reveals Are Sad

Finding out our rainbow babies' genders was complicated. I mean, not biologically (and please know that I'm not trying to be political here). All I mean is, it wasn't in my control. At this point, genetically speaking, it was what it was. But there were so many feelings behind it.

I always envisioned Chase having a little sister. Probably mostly because I am a little sister to an older brother. I also envisioned them both being alive and playing together. When I found out that Bree was going to be our little girl, I found comfort that Chase was going to have his little sister. But I was sad for her, too (and for Marcus and I, but I feel like that theme has been pretty well established). She wasn't going to have her big brother keeping her out of trouble or letting her play with his toys just so she wouldn't cry. Her big brother wouldn't be critiquing future boyfriends or kicking her to the back seat of the car when he wanted to give his new girlfriend a ride home from school (a scenario that hits close to home). I moved forward trying to mother two children in one, our little sister and our oldest child (to the eyes of strangers).

I wasn't putting undue pressure on myself to do this. I needed to do this. Holding onto both identities meant that, for me, I was including all my kids. For Bree, I was giving her the opportunity to feel all that she was. So yes, it was a lot, but it couldn't be any different.

When I was pregnant with Chase, Marcus and I knew we were having a boy. Some parents are big into being surprised and not wanting to find out the gender of the baby until they're born. I like that idea. There was a time (before Chase died) when I thought, I would want to be surprised if Chase had a sibling. But that theory went out the window when he died. No one ever says, "She's pretty emotionally unstable. You know what she'd really benefit from? A surprise!"

I remember going to get our ultrasound when I was pregnant with Matthew. As the medical assistant was walking us to our room, she asked if she should let the doctor know that we wanted to keep the gender a secret. I told her that was a definite "no" and that we'd like to find out now. She tried to encourage me to change my mind.

"Oh come on, it'll be fun! You could do one of those fun gender reveals! We could write it down for you on a piece of paper and put it in an envelope. You could take the envelope to a bakery and they could put food coloring on the inside of the cake or something."

Excellent idea—that we will not be doing. Definite hard pass. I refrained from making things horribly uncomfortable for this cute twentysomething in scrubs, and replied with a more stern "no, thank you" and an awkward smile.

Marcus and I were sitting in our car in the parking lot of the ultrasound office when we called our parents to tell them that Matthew was a boy. I cried. Oh man, I cried. If you had asked me back then what I was crying about, I don't think I could have told you. At least not using anything that resembled complete sentences. Okay, maybe a one-word sentence. Everything. I was crying about everything.

It's such a dynamic feeling having a baby the same sex as their sibling who died and a child whom you never imagined being. I'd say it's unexplainable, but I'm writing a book, so if I'm going to explain it, now is the time.

Just thinking about having another little baby boy felt like it was almost too much for my heart. It felt so heavy. There was definitely joy, but it took a little while for that joy to grow into something bigger than the accompanying sadness.

I hate admitting that I immediately thought of Chase when I heard the words "it's a boy." It was only seconds and then my thoughts shifted to this new little boy, imagining what it would be like to have him in my arms. That thought lasted just long enough though to make way for my next feeling—guilt. My youngest son deserved his own place in this world. I shouldn't be thinking about his brother at the same time. I know it's not a stretch that I made the connection, but I didn't like it.

I wondered what other people would think when they heard the news of another little boy. I'm a people pleaser, remember? I played out their comments in my head. If I could get ahead of all the possible scenarios, maybe their comments wouldn't hurt so much.

"Oh, thank goodness, you get to have your boy again."

"Oh good, now you won't have to be so sad anymore."

"I hope you give Chase's little brother his own individuality and you don't try to compare him to his big brother."

I realize these are some pretty big thoughts. I honestly don't know if anyone had them, other than me. I was so worried about the possibilities of these narratives that I actually gave them enough weight to put additional pressure on myself trying to do things just right. My priority list went something like this:

Make people happy.

Raise well-rounded babies after child loss.

Address your own happiness if you still have time.

I was already counting the ways that I could mess up Bree and Matthew's childhood. If I talked too much about Chase, they would feel like they had to compete with a shadow. Chase would always be the sibling with straight As who couldn't mess up. And yes, I was having these thoughts *before they were even born.* I think I've said this before, but this feels like a good time to pause and confirm that yes, I do have a tendency to exhaust myself with my own thoughts. And not to fast forward too far ahead, but on the off chance that I'm giving you heart palpitations for things you haven't already thought of, all of these worries have proved to be completely unwarranted and preposterous. So you stop it right now.

Special Delivery

Every delivery is different.

With Chase, my water broke and I was in the hospital for several days before I even started pushing. I pushed for hours until the little blood vessels in my neck made their way to the surface. There were lots of different nurses coming in and out.

With Bree and Matthew, they arrived within a day of entering the hospital and I pushed for ten minutes or less. The nurses were attentive but they also let me have plenty of quiet time. No, I wasn't so completely zen that I jumped in the tub for a waterbirth, but things were calm for me.

When we walked into our delivery room, Marcus placed Chase's picture on the ledge of the whiteboard hanging on the wall. We took a moment to look at the picture to see how the placement felt. This is literally the only time I've ever practiced feng shui. It felt as good as it could considering he shouldn't be a picture on the ledge. He should be back at our house, staying with his grandparents, while mom and dad were welcoming his sibling into the world.

Instead, his picture was a conversation starter with the nurses when they walked into the room to ask how I was feeling.

These nurses really do see it all. I didn't have to brace myself for any sad eyes, a surprised look, or an awkward conversation riddled with lots of "I'm sorry"s. I'm pretty sure many of them have experienced a mother losing her baby more than I had.

The nurses were there when Bree arrived crying and Matthew was silent. These kids were different from the beginning, but I was the same. Marcus and I both were. We were so scared. As the nurses stood over them giving them their first check-up, I was bracing myself that one of the nurses would turn around and give the doctor a look that says, "There's a problem." *Suspected chromosomal abnormality.* That's what the autopsy had said.

The nurses never gave us a look. Instead, with each birth, they walked over and handed me my baby. I wish I could say that their arrivals brought the same flood of tears as when Chase was born. There were tears, but they weren't the same. Chase's tears were a release. We felt relieved that he'd finally arrived and we were overjoyed for the next chapter to begin. The tears after Bree and Matthew's births were tears of "we've made it this far" and an emotional plea to make it even further.

When we moved down to the recovery room, I was still on edge. There's a buzzer in the room in case you or the baby need medical assistance. You can press it and a nurse will come in to help. I was not shy about using it. I hit that button like an overzealous contestant on *Family Feud*; I pressed it before I even knew what I wanted to say. Bree had really bad reflux. With every aggressive spit-up I couldn't help but think about the infrequency of Chase's bowel movements and the autopsy notes about his rectum that was "markedly dilated." Maybe the genetic abnormality has something to do with digestion? A part of me was on heightened alert for her and another part of me was still looking for answers for Chase. If I'm sticking with the game show analogy, this piece of me that was still looking for answers was like a contestant on *Wheel of Fortune*. "I'd like to solve the puzzle, Pat." I wanted so badly to solve the puzzle. At one point the nurses and the doctor on call took Bree for observation. I'm not sure if they were as concerned as I was or they just wanted a break from the buzzer. Bree was okay and they brought her back to me with reassurance. I absorbed as much positive feedback as my fragile heart would allow, but I was glad to be back together.

A Home for Babies and Trauma

I'd like to say that when we checked out of the hospital we left all of our worries and my terrible game show references there, but I can't. At least not the worries. A sleeping baby used to be comforting, but nap times were now unnerving. Every time I would go in to check on Bree and Matthew lying in their crib, I'd hold my breath. Marcus and I admitted to each other on several occasions (too many to count, actually) that we held out our hand and touched their tiny baby chests to make sure they were still breathing. If they looked peaceful we would initially think it's because they had just passed away. I remembered how Chase's little body felt when we said goodbye. As my hand would stretch out to reach their onesies, I wondered if they'd feel cool, too. It was always a relief to feel their warmth or see a twitch from their eyelids for being so rudely interrupted from their slumber. If Marcus was the one to check on them, I'd be waiting rather impatiently until he got back. I envisioned hearing his voice from the nursery telling me our baby was gone again.

It's not until recently, a decade later, that I've started wondering if the experiences I went through surrounding Chase's death have contributed to my anxiety. Would I be as anxious as I am today if I hadn't gone through losing Chase? I know there's no way to know for sure, but these are probably pretty reasonable questions to sit with. If you're reading this and thinking, "Um, ya think?!," don't fault a girl for being slightly behind the learning curve. I'm an overthinker, remember? It tends to lead me in a more circular direction than I'd like.

I also ask myself why I fight so hard to ignore the possibility that these rough moments in my life have impacted the person I am today in ways I don't even realize. Thank you, societal pressure, for not-so-subtly making me feel like I have to be okay (*enough time has passed...he was only a baby...death is a part of life. Yeah, whatever*).

For the first time ever I'm going to say it. Er, write it. Having my baby die was traumatic.

I have experienced trauma. Why is that so hard to say? Honestly, it makes me feel like I'm being dramatic, like it's my get outta jail free card. "It's not my fault, it's the trauma." But honestly, if I'm so proud of so many pieces of me after Chase died, it makes sense that I'd still be a little squeamish about some other pieces that I'm not so fond of. And yes, I realize I'm using the word "squeamish" in place of "traumatized." If this is the first time I'm admitting it, give me some time to embrace all the words.

The whole experience of losing someone sucks—big time. There's no "I'm Sorry for Your Loss" card that says "I'm so sorry, but look at how much better all aspects of your life are now." If there is, here's a helpful tip: *don't buy it for anyone, under any circumstance*. Not even for your archnemesis.

Sometimes, compartmentalizing things can be helpful. That happened then, *but* this is me now. Trust me, I've made plenty o' bad decisions that I'd like to move on from. Can we switch things up just a little bit though?

How about, that happened then *so* this is me now? I kinda like me now. Actually, wait, I'm not going to downplay it—I *really* like me now. It's been exhausting to try and convince myself that I haven't been shaped by *all* the details of that day, June 27, 2013; but my son's death (more generally speaking) has shaped who I am. It just seems weird and exhausting to pick and choose what has made me who I am. For example, I could say, "This part is good, but this part is bad so I'm just going to ignore that." So here I am, awkwardly talking about all of it. And giving myself, and you, a little tough love, I suppose. Don't do what I did for way too long. Don't spend the time and energy trying to filter the pieces of your tragedy. Don't downplay the particularly sad parts in order to convince yourself, or others, that you're doing "fine." Take it from me—doing all of that is emotionally exhausting. It's okay to hold all the details and surprisingly still be fine. It's not all beautiful, but it's all contributed to the beautiful person you are.

You don't have to hold onto everything so tightly if you don't want to. By all means, please, please, *please* release it if it'll make you feel better. But also recognize that all the pieces of your story are important in the grand scheme of things.

As the saying goes, we grow wiser with age. There's also a saying that age is just a number. So if the number itself isn't giving us anything, then the wisdom we gain is from our experiences. *All* of our experiences. The happy, the sad, the life, the death, the gains, the losses, the laughter, and the tears. All of it makes us who we are now.

My Own Feelings about Rainbows

When I Google "rainbow babies," there are so many results of cute onesies and colorful baby photo shoot ideas. I've had both of these, but these tangible gifts don't capture the complexity of emotions when you have a rainbow baby.

On the other side of hope there is a heaping pile of fear. Does "epic proportions" have an actual size? Because it would be that. Maybe that's why "rainbow" is the perfect name, because rainbows can be so expansive.

Popular definition says there was a storm that made way for my rainbows. I need to be very clear here though: Chase is in no way my storm. Not even on the day he died. The fear that comes from losing love, as well as that struggle to hold onto hope when fear, anger, and sadness all have invitations to the same party— well, *that* can bring with it quite the emotional cloud. Early on in my grief, I would get frustrated when the cloud showed up again. I would try to fight it out of the way. *It's not the right time for tears. Ignore it, you should be happy right now.* Now I know that this cloud will always come and go and it coexists with my rainbows and my new joys. My rainbows haven't made me pain-proof, but they sure as heck make the journey through the rough patches a lot brighter.

LOSING CHASE WAS THE catalyst that finally pushed Marcus to go back to school to become a teacher. This wasn't a dartboard decision. Not finishing college and not picking the career he'd always wanted were regrets I'd heard about since before we were married. Life had just kinda taken over, and at some point he felt it was just too late. Nothing like some trauma and a toxic work environment to put things into perspective. It didn't feel like a choice. It felt like there was no other option. He *needed* to do what he loved. If he didn't, I think we were both afraid that despair is just where we would acceptingly sit for the foreseeable future.

So for the four years after Chase died, we incorporated some of our retired vocabulary back into the mix: Night class. Group project. Proofread. Syllabus. Bree was only a few months old when school started, and Marcus graduated and got his teaching job when Matthew was a few years old. It wasn't at all easy but we told ourselves we'd been through harder times. It's amazing the amount of work you'll sign up for when the other option is continuing to feel broken and stuck.

Marcus wasn't the only one going through a chaotic career shift. A few months after Chase passed away, the company I work for had entered into negotiations for an acquisition. This meant lots of late nights at the office for me. Yes, I probably could have told my manager and coworkers that this workload was too heavy of a lift for me at the time, but the timing was perfect in that I was looking for a way to avoid my emotions.

Probably not the healthiest choice (*hello, avoidance!*), and this left Marcus grieving alone a lot of the time. Grief is selfish, remember? The company's acquisition closed and the following years continued to be chaotic. They still are.

So, with Marcus just starting his new career and me still trying to find footing on the swaying corporate ladder, there was one big decision we'd have to make. What do we do about daycare for Bree and then Matthew?

Before I was even pregnant again, our early conversations were about how to live in our current California conditions on a teacher's salary. It was a frustrating discussion to nowhere. The math didn't work and I wasn't sure I wanted to be a stay-at-home mom. Is it what I wanted, or was it purely a fear-based option? I didn't know. We avoided the topic completely while I was pregnant with Bree. It took more emotional energy than what we could give at the time. I was too busy hyperventilating over at-home heartbeat monitors, remember?

The Difficult Search

When Bree was about two months old, we started the search. I had two more months before I'd be wrapped up with my employee parental leave and my mom would be traveling back home after several weeks of free daycare. I requested a list of registered daycare providers from the county and put my stalking skills to good use.

If the list provided an address, I Googled the street view. If the street view consisted of a rusty old truck parked on the front lawn, it was a hard pass. If the still frames caught pictures of smiling children, I put them on the "definite maybe" list. Great reviews from clients got you a spot on the "let's schedule an awkward meeting" list.

I was so nervous for that first meeting. It was with two sisters who had their own small at-home daycare. With Marcus carrying a sleeping Bree in her car seat, we arrived for a tour of their home. It was clean and, as far as childcare providers go, they seemed very nurturing and responsible. But that's not always enough. Not anymore, anyway.

They led us to a garden in the backyard where the kids were growing vegetables. There was lots of room for playing in a nearby sandbox and plenty of shade (Bree had not inherited Marcus's Portuguese complexion). It all seemed very zen. The house was only a few blocks from the beach, so that probably helped. For a brief moment I thought maybe I should go here. The sisters walked us down the hallway and brought us into the bedroom where Bree would be taking her naps. Okay, here we go.

I could feel the weight of this moment with every step we took toward that room. I was walking forward, but my mind was envisioning me turning around and running to the car parked out front. This felt like as good a time as any to have a meltdown. Actually, not really, but regardless of what I wanted, this is where said meltdown occurred.

Having someone else watch your child can be a little nerve-wracking for parents even if everything goes well. You conduct a few interviews, review some logistics, get a "good feeling," and then you entrust this person with your child's life.

It's like a trust fall. Have you ever done one of those? They used to be a staple at childhood overnight camps. Maybe even a requirement. It's where you turn your back to your partner, stretch out your arms, and slowly lean back. Just before you feel like you're going to hit the ground, your partner stretches out their arms to catch you.

When you go through a traumatic event it's like not being caught by your partner during a trust fall. You simply hit the ground—*really freakin' hard*. You're then swallowed by the confusion of it all, trying to figure out how it all went so wrong.

I didn't end up running to the car, but I did want to be transparent about what we were bringing to the table, besides the required child that needed watching. We were talking with the ladies about the room set-up and how many cribs they had. I believe it was Marcus who asked about their use of baby monitors. This seemed like as good a time as any, right? Cue meltdown.

I started to tell them about Chase and why selecting child care was challenging for us and why we might seem to be asking more questions than they usually receive from their parents. I actually think I can be too breezy at times, so maybe we were asking the right amount of questions and it only felt overboard to us. But do all parents ask their questions while wiping snot from their nose and talking about how their oldest son died? They were understandably caught a little off guard but they were so kind, offering condolences and assuring us that Bree would be well taken care of.

We didn't end up signing up with the sisters. No, not because they broke up with us. Their location wasn't ideal for the logistics of drop-off and pick-up. We signed up with another provider who was actually only a few blocks from our house. She clicked the logistics box and she had been established for years. When the time came to tell her about Chase, she was actually already familiar with our story. I suppose word had traveled amongst providers in our smaller town. It was comforting that she didn't shy away from the conversation. Aa an added bonus, since I'd already cried at a few of the interviews, my eyes remained shockingly dry at this one.

With just a few weeks to go before I would be going back to work, there was a little bit of relief that we had this piece figured out. Or at least we thought it was settled until our new provider called us a week later to tell us that her husband was offered a new job and they were going to be moving out of state. Wonderful. And by wonderful, I mean not so much.

What were we going to do now? How were we going to find someone again? Someone who loved our children as much as we did. Someone who gave them love while we were away. How were we going to find someone again like Brenda?

That was the exact issue—we were spending so much time trying to find someone *like* Brenda. So, why not ask Brenda?

Chase's Ball

We had talked with her a few times in the year after Chase died. For months I couldn't talk to her. It was too much for me. I wasn't angry, I just didn't have the capacity for my pain and hers. It took me back to that day as we sat on her staircase, feeling my own pain set in and watching hers become all-consuming. The first time that I called her was to tell her we were pregnant with Bree. I know it was healing for my heart, so I thought maybe it would be for hers too. We didn't speak on a regular basis but we had touched base over time. Things didn't feel as heavy now as they did then, and there was a part of me now that actually felt that I needed her. I just wasn't sure exactly how much and in what capacity. Would it be just to chat for an hour or would it become more than that?

Marcus and I were caught up in thinking that we couldn't possibly go back to the home where Chase died. That would just be too much. But would it?

I told Marcus it wouldn't hurt to at least ask Brenda if she had an opening at her daycare. If she didn't, then we'd know to keep looking. I texted her and she got back to me quickly saying that she did have an opening. We scheduled a time to go over to her house.

There were no set expectations with this meeting. We didn't know how we'd feel going back to her house. We didn't know how she'd react to seeing us. For the past year we had been on our own healing journeys and maybe we had headed off in different directions. After all, we were all different people by now. We were understandably forever changed.

Marcus and I arrived with Bree. As we rounded the corner to Brenda's street I think Marcus and I were both holding our breath. The last time we were there, there were police vehicles, lots of suits and uniforms, and a crowd of neighbors forming. This time, it was about 5:30 p.m. and the street was quiet. Sighs of relief.

I was looking forward to introducing Bree to Brenda. Brenda had the superpower of making every child feel completely loved. I was confident that Chase felt that love wholeheartedly and the idea of sharing that kind of love with Bree seemed, well, nice.

Chase didn't gain his wings because of something that Brenda did or didn't do. If that was the case, I was just as much at fault.

I was standing on the front porch with the infant carrier. The last time I did this was the last morning I had with Chase. I looked down at Bree the same way I did with Chase.

The door opened and Brenda welcomed us into her home with hugs and smiles. Here we go—again.

We made our way down the stairs inside to where the daycare was. The same staircase where Marcus first succumbed to his grief and the strong-armed officer. Stepping off the stairs, the first thing we noticed was that the couch was still there. The one Marcus and I had sat on, holding Chase for the last time. Marcus and I decided to take a seat on the floor next to Bree's carrier instead. Brenda's husband came downstairs to join us and we welcomed him with hugs too.

Brenda's daycare still closed at 5:00 p.m. and we had arrived closer to 5:30. I was surprised to see a little boy still playing quietly downstairs. Brenda explained that the mom was running late from work. I didn't mind.

We caught up like old friends. We asked how our families were doing, how the daycare was, and then talked about our little Miss Bree. Brenda asked how the pregnancy had been and what kind of baby Bree was. We didn't get into any heavy emotional discussions. I think we all wanted to use this time to share with each other that we were all doing okay. None of us were getting tripped up in a lie. We were all doing okay. I'm sure if one of us had started down the path of sharing our struggles over the past year, we could have all had a story or two (more like twenty-five), but that's not why we were there.

We were focused on how it felt being back here. Could we be here again every day? Was this the best fit for us, for Brenda and her family, and for Bree?

As we continued to talk and catch up, the little boy who was waiting for his mom continued to play. He would go up and down the Little Tikes plastic slide, loving the attention when we'd give him overly exaggerated smiles for his dedication.

At one point the boy lost hold of a ball he was playing with. The ball looked like a sphere of dark blue honeycomb with a few of the waffle holes being filled in with clear plastic rattles and primary colored beads.

The ball rolled across the floor and tapped me on the foot. I looked down and I just knew it. It was Chase's ball.

We left a few things at Brenda's house after Chase died. My parents had gone back to retrieve our infant carrier, but we'd left formula and some smaller items. It was too hard at the time to think about going back for them. Chase loved playing with his ball and I had brought it to daycare with him one day.

I looked over at Marcus and I picked it up. The little boy looked at me, probably slightly frustrated that I didn't just toss it back to him right away. I eventually did. I'm not sure if Brenda could tell what I was thinking. We didn't talk about it, but she spoke up to tell me that I could have the ball.

A year earlier I couldn't go back for the ball. Now I was taking it as a sign that I needed to keep coming back. It was at that moment that I felt comfort come over me. We had said goodbye just a few feet away from where we were sitting, but Chase was still here. All this time he was helping me heal, but he was here too, helping Brenda and her family also. He was watching over this home and the kids who continued to come here. If Bree was here, her big brother would watch over her. I not only wanted her to be here, I felt that she needed to be here. I told Brenda I wanted her to keep the ball.

Marcus, Bree, and I left Brenda's house, politely saying that we'd think about it. She wasn't looking for commitment either. Once Marcus and I were out of earshot, we immediately started talking about the ball. We had both felt something special at that moment. We didn't have to politely think about anything. A short time later we told Brenda we'd love to come back to her daycare if she'd have us. She welcomed us without hesitation.

From an outsider's perspective, I often wonder if people think we're totally crazy for going back to the daycare where our son died. Maybe becoming a stay-at-home mom would have made more sense? I don't know. What I do know is that oftentimes the thing that makes the most sense about grief is the very fact that it can make no sense at all. Who should it make sense to? An outsider? There's no skin in the game for them—it doesn't have to make sense to anyone else but you. You do you.

Bree and Matthew spent the next five years going to Miss Brenda's five days a week. I'll be honest. Every day that Marcus and I rounded that street corner to pick up or drop off the kids, we thought about that last day with Chase. Brenda's neighbor was a police officer and on days he would stop by the house and park his patrol car out front, Marcus's heart would sink all over again. We should have asked the neighbor to park one street over and just walk home.

In early grief, I didn't have extra space for anything or anyone. Me and my sadness pretty much filled my cup. I'm not sure when it happened, probably just over time, but at some point I gained space. Selective space. Enough space that I chose Brenda and she chose me, too. I can't imagine that it was easy for her seeing me again. No matter how cool I am.

I saw the faces of those other daycare providers as I stood in their homes crying. I could tell them what happened and try to explain (it felt like I had to justify) why I'm so fragile, but they'd never truly understand it. I wanted to be understood. I needed to be understood.

I wanted to talk to someone who understood firsthand how cool Chase was. Someone who had enjoyed his little belly laugh like I had. Someone who wasn't afraid to talk to Bree and Matthew about their older brother, and who enjoyed the opportunity with every fiber of their being. Someone who knew, as much as an outsider to the grief-stricken can, how fragile I really was.

So as hard as it was to go back to Chase's daycare, it had proved to be so much harder not to.

Next time you're asking yourself what the right thing to do in grief is, use me as an example. It's okay to sit in indecision. I'd say it's a necessity. But when something speaks to you, just listen. It might seem messed up to others and you may even question your own sanity for thinking it's even a possibility. But if you sit with it long enough and your heart starts to feel warm about it, you're not crazy and you've already found your answer.

ELEVEN - JUGGLING RAINBOWS AND BIG FEELINGS

WORRY.
Fear.
Panic.
Uncertainty.
Joy.
Appreciation.
Wholeness.
Love.
Remembrance.

Raising children after losing a child is different. How is it different? Okay, you got me. I actually have no idea because I don't know anything different. What I do know is that I carry around these big feelings and I make choices that a lot of the time I can only attribute to my experience of losing Chase. Our experiences lead to other experiences. Our lives are shaped by their biggest impacts. It's not wrong or right, although your big feelings might say otherwise sometimes. It just is. Raising Bree and Matthew is my most savored experience, shaped by my big feelings and my experiences with Chase—his life and his death.

Worry. Fear. Panic. Uncertainty.

When Bree was about one and a half years old, she got sick. It was a case of really bad snot, a fever, and a cough. I was telling myself it was all routine stuff, but in the background I was Googling coughing sounds and following Marcus around the house playing sound bites and asking, "Do you think she sounds like this?" My pacing subsided momentarily so I could fold laundry and stare at Bree, who was sitting on our bed amongst freshly dried clothes. I let Marcus wander off to another room unattended.

Bree began again with another coughing spell and it sounded so painful. Just as soon as she started coughing though, she stopped. She was unintentionally quiet. Her face was turning bright red, to dark red to hints of blue as she had her mouth open trying to get air. I froze and screamed for Marcus. As soon as he came in and patted her on the back she threw up the phlegm that was blocking her airway and she was back to her normal color. I, on the other hand, was anything but back to normal.

Marcus and I were both worried at that moment. Our concern was totally valid and we did end up going to the emergency room for total peace of mind. However, my heightened screams didn't help the situation. Well, actually maybe they did. I was able to call for someone who could help her. It's not Bree's cough or projectile phlegm that I cling to when remembering this moment. It's the total disappointment in myself for the way I reacted. I didn't rush over to pat her on the back. I panicked.

Immediately following Bree's coughing fit, I just cried. Ugly cried. I cried because I was scared. I cried with relief. I cried because in that moment I felt that I wasn't the kind of parent who could save her child. I was the kind who panicked and just froze. I cried because I was reminded again that I wasn't as tough and numb to tragedy as I thought I was (because it had happened to me already).

I sometimes wonder what it would have been like to be the one who found Chase on that day during nap time. Would I have sprung into action like Brenda and her daughter and administered CPR and called 9-1-1? Could I have saved him? Or, at the very least, would I have been consoled by first responders for doing all the right things? Moments of fear with my children, like Bree's gnarly cough at a young age, have me thinking I would have come up short. So while I have feelings of regret for not being there for Chase, I'm also grateful it wasn't me. I don't know if I could have done better for him. Sometimes not knowing is okay with me.

Joy. Appreciation.

I haven't sent out a family Christmas card since before Chase was born. All I think about is that last family photo session the week before Chase died. Those were supposed to be pictures we could use for that year's card that never came. It's become a sticking point for me. To clarify, I have taken lots and been in lots of family pictures over the years. Bree and Matthew are always peppered to take "just one more" and the progression of my aging fine lines and wrinkles is bountifully documented, *thankyouverymuch*. I just don't go through the exercise of printing them out, filling out an envelope, and slapping a stamp on it—essentially the part that makes the photo for other people.

When we have a planned family photo session, we hold a star in the picture for Chase. We had a banner in his nursery that claimed him as our "All Star." Sometimes, the kids will hold a star ornament or we'll take down one of our star decorations from the wall of our home and prop it up somewhere in the photo.

In more recent years, we've taken a few of the family photos without the star. As much as I don't like to admit it, some of the times it was missing because we forgot to pick it up before the photographer started snapping away. Sometimes I leave it out on purpose just to see how it feels. How does it feel? Well, not good.

My grandma used to tell me that "hate" is a strong word, but sorry, Grandma, I gotta say I hate it. All of it. I hate that it's my choice to put his symbolic stand-in in the picture or not. What I really hate though is that it's a tangible token and not my son. Sometimes having the star in the picture just stings. So I put it in a little bit of a time-out and I sit in the present. When it's me and Marcus, Bree, and Matthew, smiling. Smiling as I hold onto the memories of Chase. Smiling as I miss him. Smiling as I feel joy and gratitude to be able to enjoy the moment with Bree and Matthew.

Smiling as...smiling as...smiling as.

It's smiling as I figure out how mothering in Heaven and on Earth all works together for me and for my family. It's never been a question of how to grieve and then smile. This is not a linear path where you go from one and onto the other. Have you ever had a necklace chain that has managed to get itself into knots? It's like that. It's messy. It requires patience. There's not just one way to solve it.

Sometimes you gotta loop back around to where you've already been to feel untangled. Sometimes you gotta take a break to be able to come back and see it all with a bit more hope and confidence. Yes, it's a little bit tangled up but it all makes something whole, and there's relief that it's all still connected and you haven't lost any of the pieces.

Raising my kids on Earth and honoring my son in Heaven is my necklace. It makes me whole.

Love. Remembrance.

Early introductions to grief offer an opportunity to raise empathetic children.

When my daughter was in kindergarten I had my first parent-teacher conference. I sat in the tiny chair as her teacher recapped how Bree was doing in the classroom (great, by the way). At the end of her spiel her teacher asked if I had any questions or concerns we hadn't talked about. I took the opportunity to let the teacher know that Bree has an older brother who had passed away before she was born. I explained that I didn't know if it had come up in the classroom, but that we all talk openly about Chase at home, so it wouldn't surprise me. Not to mention, kindergarten is very heavy on the "About Me" assignments and this is a piece of our family "About." Her teacher was very nice about my take on Share Day—I'm sure she's heard a lot about family dynamics in her line of work.

"Yeah, no, she hasn't said anything."

"Oh, okay. Great!" I said with an overabundance of positivity. Because was it great? I was kinda bummed it *hadn't* come up. Okay, fine, a lot bummed. Little kids say a lot of awkward and uncomfortable things. I feel like this would have been pretty easy pickings. Yes, the mom in me knew the right thing to say was always whatever she felt comfortable with.

What if her teacher had responded with, "Yes, she talks about her big brother all the time! I feel like I know Chase so well that I've actually added him to the class roster." Okay, I knew that wasn't going to happen. But in another life, it could have. It should have. Her teacher would know all about Chase because he would be walking onto the school campus with Bree, dropping her off at kindergarten, and then heading off to first grade. At the end of the day, he'd be meeting her back at the front gate after school so they could walk out together and wait for their notoriously late mother to pick them up.

Yes, I'm a hypocrite. I fully realize that my kids leaving their older brother out of their sibling count is the same thing as when I leave Chase out of my child count in a breezy conversation, or when I purposefully leave a star ornament out of our family photos. I don't always want to risk making the special and raw place in my heart a socially awkward moment. I imagine Bree and Matthew won't want to either. Then there's the other possibility that he honestly didn't cross Bree's mind. My kids' relationship with Chase is a lot different than mine. They never met him in person. It makes sense to me why I would inquire about an honorable mention at a parent-teacher conference, but sometimes I feel bad—reminding them to keep holding onto something they technically never even held in the first place.

Fast forward to when Bree is in second grade. I got a message from her teacher one day giving me a heads up that Bree talked about her older brother during share time. She talked to her classmates about Chase being in Heaven. Her teacher said it was all very positive and her classmates were very kind.

So. Many. Thoughts.

First one…"YES!!!!"

Next… "Oh my gosh, I hope she's doing okay, that was really brave."

Then…"I hope she didn't feel pressured to talk about him because she sees how much Mom laughs and cries talking about Chase and she's just wanting to please me. Oh, crap, she's going to grow up to be an unwavering people pleaser. She didn't have to say his name. I'm totally messing her up."

Calm down, Laura. This was *her* family photo moment. She put the star in the picture just to see how it feels. Play it cool.

Enjoy the heartwarming moment because they can't all be this warm and fuzzy.

One night, as I was tucking Bree into bed, she looked up at me all cute and cozy and asked, "Mom, do you love Chase more than me?"

Probably one of my greatest fears realized when raising kids after child loss. Comparing yourself to a child who has never done or will never do anything wrong.

After the pang of the tiny gut punch subsided, my initial response as an overthinker was that I needed to "fix this." And yes, I realize that as I was busy mapping out how to change every parenting skill I'd proudly put into my toolbox, because they clearly weren't working, Bree had probably forgotten she even asked the question and was comfortably settling into a slumber.

As moms we're encouraged to try and find the right mix of career, motherhood, physical health, emotional well-being, drive to achieve, and sense of presence. Fudge, it's exhausting. That's why I tend to lean toward my own sort of hybrid model. It's the method of fooling myself into thinking I have it together until one day I have an epic meltdown, a good cry, and then I start over. That's my "lather, rinse, repeat" model.

So now, on top of this "usual stuff," I worry about the right balance of talking about the dead. I mean, I have to worry about it, right? Because I want to talk about him a lot and the kids want to know all about their big brother. Yes, I've also wondered if it's only because I keep talking about him. Honestly, who knows? I think I'll have to wait it out until that one day when they're all grown up and opinionated, when they finally tell me all the ways in which I've messed them up.

Have you ever noticed that some older people love telling stories of their younger days? If you're around them long enough, you'll hear the same story seventy-five thousand times. As their story begins (again) with, "Have I ever told you about the time...?" you immediately think, "Here we go again." Sometimes you can't bite your tongue and you spew out the *CliffsNotes* version within thirty seconds, in hopes that you won't have to sit through the long version. Sometimes, you give the person their time to tell the story and you actually discover that there is still joy in seeing them relive their special moments. You may even feel like a total a-hole for ever trying to speed up their trip down memory lane.

Life creates these incredible moments that turn into the stories we keep in constant rotation. These special memories have a way of sticking to you. They make you smile and laugh over and over again.

Guess what? That's grief.

Grief has you talking about something (or someone) that made you so incredibly happy. But it's not only because it made you happy. It's because it's gone. Maybe not gone in the sense that the people died or something tragic happened. Maybe life just has you in a different space right now where that memory doesn't have the opportunity to play out again.

I guess what I'm trying to say is: Chase's death has turned me into an eighty-nine-year-old. I have a short time of physical memories with Chase, and sometimes I am that person who says, "Have I ever told you...?" when I know with near-certainty I've told the same versions of the story several times already.

Have I ever told you that Chase loved bath time?

Have I ever told you that Chase loved to giggle?

Have I ever told you about the first time Chase and I played peek-a-boo?

Have I ever told you that Chase loved to play with his ball?

My kids here on Earth may inevitably hear me talk about Chase more than they might want (again, they haven't said anything, but I'm going with my gut here). Sometimes it's more than I want because I can feel like I'm grasping to hold on and I hate that.

I start sharing a wonderful memory and partway through I start to feel anger seep its way around my words. I've been known to cut myself off with the *CliffsNotes* version. "My water broke just as I was climbing into bed, then...(*CliffsNotes*) some other things happened, and he was born."

My hope is that in the times my kids let me share my stories with Chase, and I'm in a right headspace to share the details, they see my joy and that helps them to feel more joy about their brother too.

Siblings compete, they love, they bicker, they support, they ignore. It kinda brings me comfort that Bree's question of "do you love him more?" falls into this group of sibling dynamics. Except, of course, for the fact that the whole physical presence piece is missing. I know, I think it's a huge piece too.

If Chase were alive and cuddled up in the bedroom next to her, would she have asked me if I love him more? Since I'm not in a court of law and I don't have to worry about the objection of hearsay, I'm going to go with 100 percent yes on this one.

So, my beautiful daughter, I don't love him more. I love him the same. I love him through my memories. The ones I'm so deeply grateful that you and I get to continue making. Mommy just likes to repeat herself.

I feel like this is a good time to apologize to those whom I've ever cut off from telling a special story from their repeat rolodex of memories. Next time you feel the urge, please tell me again. I'm listening.

EPILOGUE

S HORTLY AFTER CHASE PASSED away I was online and I found a forum for infant loss. Someone recommended that after your baby dies, you should put a piece of your baby's unwashed clothing in a Ziploc bag. If you seal it up real tight, you could hold onto their smell and revisit it whenever you need to. I thought this was a genius idea.

I quickly did my best mall-walk into Chase's quiet nursery. I grabbed a worn and unwashed onesie and the soft brown cover of his changing table. For the record, it was purchased brown. I was grieving, not gross.

I carefully folded and then quickly stuffed the soft pieces into a freezer-sized Ziploc bag and sealed it up. I was so pleased to have captured this before it was too late. Now, I could open it up and have a little piece of him whenever I needed it.

Less than a week later, on a particularly tough day, I grabbed the Ziploc bag. I opened it up, hopeful that I'd get to smell him again. I opened it up just wide enough to get my nose in the bag without letting too much of the stored smells sneak out. I was careful not to breathe into the bag or breathe too deeply that I'd steal all the smell. I took a carefully curated sniff.

Do you know what I smelled? Yup, a plastic bag. There was no scent of fresh baby butt or smell of his soft skin. I would have even settled for the stench of stale spit-up. All that I had wanted to hold onto was gone.

I didn't need a bag to tell me that he was, indeed, gone. I knew. I just didn't *want* to know yet. So instead I tortured myself with this plastic bag exercise. I don't fault myself. My heart had to try.

It's hard to try and preserve what's gone. Inevitably, grief has made me face a lot of things I don't want to. This covers some pretty big topics: pain, my own mortality, the extremely long and never-ending timeline of healing, changes in relationships, questioning how to measure my heart's capacity, wondering about my life's purpose, my relationship with God, letting go of the person I thought I'd be, embracing the person I am, appreciating the person I was, and giving myself grace as I look ahead to find out who I can still become.

I've also come to realize that being honest and awkward has infinite benefits. You're not horrible for trying to find a smile when the situation might typically call for lots of crying. Crying all the time can really take it out of you.

I once asked Marcus if it was weird that I sometimes thought the chihuahua we adopted sometime after Chase passed away was Chase reincarnated. By the look on his face I knew his answer. Yes, it was weird. But we're still married, so maybe not that weird? At the very least, he understood what I was trying to do—keep Chase in our present.

Our beautiful present. I'm so grateful for Bree and Matthew. They were born from two people who were very broken. They have grown up with grief. They have shared that they miss Chase. We've all cuddled and cried together. They have so much empathy and understanding. I see it every time they ask, "Mom, are you crying...again?" I've actually had to correct them when my tears are from laughing too hard. "No, mommy's not sad this time." That's been a great lesson to teach and a nice reminder that things are okay. More than okay. They are beautiful.

It's kind of crazy that losing can actually lead to more. If your grief is still fresh, you're probably wanting to give me a swift punch in the mouth for even bringing up this idea. But please hear me out. It's true. Through tears, there will be more smiles to come.

I will never be okay that Chase died. But I am grateful for the good that has happened in my life since he left (never *because* he left). I know with all of my being that he has played a part in every piece of it.

He has shown and taught me so much since his life ended. He was small and plump, but his impact remains enormous and infinite. In that regard, there wasn't an end. Like the process of writing this book, there's just the next chapter and he's always in it. I don't need a Ziploc bag of smells to feel that.

You Are Already Making the Masterpiece

One night, shortly after Chase passed away, I met the girls in my moms' group at a restaurant. As we were sitting there talking, one of the girls was recounting something they had done recently to help another child loss mom. I was in awe.

I laid myself out on an empty restaurant bench and flopped my arms over my face, as a declaration of defeat. "I don't know how you do it. I don't think I'll ever be able to help someone else. I can't even help myself."

Sometimes it's hard to know whether you're helping yourself through loss, or if it's just that enough time has passed and you've made your way through the natural progression of things.

It's been a decade of living since I've held Chase. The stories and moments I've shared in this book are still so clear to me. It's like getting stung by that bee I mentioned in the introduction. I remember the wheres and whens of being stung and I'm able to talk more easily about it now because it all stings a little bit less.

It doesn't stop me anymore from wanting to go out in public or refusing to get out of bed. The grief isn't as loud and for that I'm grateful. I'm also grateful for the work I've done to get here. You should be too. I repeat, *you should be too.* You, my friend, are helping yourself even when it doesn't feel like it.

You are here. Your world's most beautiful gift was taken away, and you are still here. You are doing it. Sure, the passing of time is helpful. I love a good fast-forward button, but your resilience and your relationship with grief and your path to creating your life is a masterpiece only you can paint.

Your picture starts out with some structural elements—life's most treasured gift taken too soon, beautiful memories, and the deepest pain. Everything else is for you to fill in.

Getting out of bed.

Making decisions.

Stepping back outside.

Going to work.

Getting pregnant again through pain.

Finding and filtering friendships.

Making changes that feel right for you.

Evaluating or straight-up ignoring outside opinions.

Leaning into the awkward.

Relentlessly holding onto the humor.

These are the scribbles to your masterpiece. Yes, even those ones that slip off the page and onto your desk—especially those.

OUR FAMILY—INCLUDING CHASE'S STAR
Circa 2021

ACKNOWLEDGMENTS

MENTIONED IT BRIEFLY BEFORE, but it's true—this book wouldn't be what it is if I had tried to write it any earlier. I not only had to sort through my own feelings (not done yet, but definitely more refined), but I truly believe that my heart had to open (back) up enough to let a lot of special people in. I'm so incredibly grateful for the encouragement, empathy, love, patience, constructive feedback, hugs, tears, laughs, and cheers over these past few years.

To Marcus, Love, for your strategically placed sticky notes of encouragement. For holding me accountable and for being ready with 6:00 a.m. hugs, after I'd already been writing for over an hour. My tears, even if almost dry, were a subtle hint I just needed them. Thank you for knowing I could do it before I ever did. You are my coach, my best friend, and my teammate. I love you with all of my heart!

To Bree and Matthew, thank you for always asking me, "How's your book going?" Thank you for understanding that writing this is something Mom is very proud of. I hope it brings more to your lives than I can ever imagine and it encourages you to create what's in your heart no matter how out of reach it may seem. Find those who lift you up and realize your potential. You deserve the world.

To my parents, thank you for life and for nurturing the writer in me from an early age. Definitely not how we planned the pages, but I think they're even more special than we thought possible. I appreciate all you've done and continue to do for me—there will never be enough pages.

To all of my extended family and friends who have checked in and who have said you can't wait to read it—my tears (yes, more) are from the overabundance of love you have shown me. Thank you (insert inappropriate hugs here).

To Kelly, thank you for placing me on a path to get it done and for your coaching and friendship during the writing process.

To all of the authors and experts who I connected with at that first workshop and beyond through Rising Authors, thank you for continuing to inspire me by putting the creative process and people first—your beautiful professionalism and passion in the wake of uncertainty make me want to be the best version of myself.

To Vi, thank you for your help, care, and understanding with finding a title that fit this next right step—not Juggling, but Wishing.

To Nicole and Copper Mountain Books, plainly put, we were meant to be together. It wasn't coincidence that we found each other. Thank you for sticking with me in uncertain times, with nothing but a messy draft and a drive to get things done. You are simply the best!

To all of us who have lost a child and are mothering in Heaven or on Earth—thank you for being a community that understands, embraces laughter, and weaves a special strength through it all. The world needs all of our stories.

.

www.ingramcontent.com/pod-product-compliance
Lightning Source LLC
Chambersburg PA
CBHW031514120626
46545CB00005B/1875